THE LOST LEADER

2

MICK IMLAH  ∼  The Lost Leader

faber and faber

First published in 2008
by Faber and Faber Limited
3 Queen Square London WC1N 3AU

Typeset by Faber and Faber Limited
Printed in England by T. J. International Ltd, Padstow, Cornwall
Printed on FSC accredited material

A CIP record for this book
is available from the British Library

ISBN 978-0-571-24307-5

**FSC**

**Mixed Sources**
Product group from well-managed
forests and other controlled sources

Cert no. SGS-COC-2482
www.fsc.org
© 1996 Forest Stewardship Council

10  9  8  7  6  5

... *no poet in Scotland now can take as his inspiration the folk impulse that created the ballads, the people's songs, and the legends of Mary Stuart and Prince Charlie. He has no choice but to be at once more individual and less local.*

EDWIN MUIR, *Scottish Journey*, 1935

# Contents

# THE LOST LEADER

# Muck

(AD)

Hey, we were only semi-literate
ourselves: we meant to head for Mull, not
where the blessed Kevin miscarried us,
a rank bad place with no words at all.

It was about the year dot – before
MacBrayne and the broken ice; before
Colum and Camelot, whose annals skate
over our failed attempt on Muck –

when the call came (I didn't hear it)
to rid ourselves of the Ulster roof-
and-cake mentality, and work abroad.
So we did go, in wash-tub coracles,

and hauled ashore for an hour or so, on a
black upturned platter of rock, stained
with sea-lichen and scummy pools
of barge flies and crab water.

No trees, then. No welcoming men
or women either. But out on a spur's end
we spotted a sham temple – being a few
upright poles fashioned from driftwood, which

when we straggled over to them, seemed,
without a text or rune to vent their purpose,
to have their say in fish. ('That's one
of our symbols,' said Kevin, slowly.)

∾

The first was crude, like holy rood,
a shark hung where the Christ might be.
The crossbeam of the second, wavy,
White and queasy, was split three times

by dolphins' leaps and falls; while each
of the mounting horizontals of the next,
carved with a rogue's dash or abandon,
was a fish-beam: the worst given the arc

of a catfish – though closer to, we saw
how this was worked from a lower jaw,
the bass jaw of an ox. These three might seem
the project of a class of kids; except

for the cunning which had placed the group
of crosses, if we call them crosses,
in silhouette, against the setting sun,
her *lux in embro*; or the paler moon.

The fourth was set apart. It wore
the red back half of a toy tractor, fixed
to the neck of a pole; and strapped to the spine,
a thermos, meant to last the afternoon . . .

– the cairn beneath it had been plugged, once,
with a plastic helmet – that was bleached by now
from orange to lime or yellow; and over the whole
was thrown a mongrel dress of fishnet and floats.

∼

K saw a fifth, with his second sight,
and wasn't telling. Only, 'Back to the boats! –
It's no good, we brought the word of God
to those in hiding here, and they don't want it!'

[4]

(So we sounded in reply the child's note
of feigned frustration, masking the relief
our code forbids us to have felt, or
having felt, express.) Till as we sucked

our wicker boats and heels clear of their shingle,
he struck up from the front, bellowing out
Our Founder's Lesson, 'Study the Mountains' (strange
how the borrowed prose would fill him full of himself) –

'*Study the mountains; then when you fancy
that you know the mountains, you can learn the stars.*'
(Just then, Kevin, none of us rowing could
see past the grimed horizon of your neck;

and as the squall got up, you couldn't hear
half that we aimed in reply; until with the double
beating of salt and rain on our hands and face
we sank back in the bee-shape; kept at the oars.

But we will expect something to sustain us,
soon, beyond the Plough and the Sperrins.
In the meantime, here's to the gay goddess
Astarté – mother of false starts!)

# The Prophecies

*1  Of the book which fell into the water-vessel*

ONE day, as he was staring into the hall-fire
with such sadness, that the serving brethren
redoubled their normal silence – he caught sight
in a corner of the youth Lugbe, from the clan Cummin,
reading a book, and suddenly said to him,
not in a threatening way, 'Take care, my son,
for it seems that the book you are reading is about
to fall into a vessel full of water.'

And so it proved: for when in time the boy
stood up to fetch a candle, he seemed to forget
the prophetic warning, and as he passed by
one of the saint's more senior men the book
slipped from under his arm, and lo! it was text-
down in the foot-bath, which was full of water.

*2  Similar, of the Thuringian inkhorn*

ONE day, when a shout went up on the far side
of the Sound of Hy, the saint, who had made for himself
an hour apart in his room, to meditate,
grew aware of the shout, and said, 'The man who is shouting
beyond the Sound is not of very sharp wit,
since when he comes knocking here today
for his food, or a spiritual lesson, he will surely
upset my Thuringian inkhorn, and spill the ink.'

This put his monks in a quandary, – whether
to bring the thing on, or to prevent it;
and some were busy, and some were standing still
the moment the shouter arrived: who in his haste
to embrace the saint, brushed the desk with a trailing
sleeve and we all had to write about it.

## 3  Of the dead letter

ONE day Baithene, his old attendant, asked him:
'Could you spare a learned brother to read the psalter
your servant has written, and correct it?' To which
the saint replied: 'Why give my staff the trouble?
I daresay that in this psalter of yours, there is not
one word or letter too many; on the other hand,
look again at the work, and you will find
that everywhere the vowel 'i' is omitted!'

Now when Baithene went back to the manuscript,
and checked it over, he found to his amazement
that in his absence some tick had gone over
his stuff and with a blue pencil scored out
every sentence in the first person, including
the entire intro and the acknowledgements.

## 4  Of a future book

Of course it got better, when he grew older
and sitting at supper was less apt to see
Judas in everyone's face at his shoulder:
'the wheels', as he put it, 'secure on the axle',
our wagon was 'fit to roam into the future'.

Thus, once, he emerged from a session, the dark
of his eyes rolled back from view – a trick he had –
and spoke of a small, black, impending book:

*The Life of St Columba, Founder of Hy*
by Adam something – many an abbot later –
in Penguin Classics, nineteen ninety-nine.
And now as he shared the vision he felt, he said,
a warm, delicious tingle and flush of the veins
as if he had been ravished by who knows whom.

# I

Elderly, veiny, eccentric: our guide, running
a leak from his nose, with not enough coat

to keep out the flat rain or hail of Iona,
is 'taking the story on from Columba'.

For here, as our Lord's first millennium bumped
on its dark philological bottom or *nadir*,

they carried the freezing body of Fergus Mor,
crawled through the winter to give him grace;

Fergus, whose ancestral line or graveway
appears as a series of pock marks in the grass.

*Is nothing sacred? Not the burial ground
of the ur-kings, the first Scots known by name?*

'. . . And Fergus's son was Domangart Macfergus;
and he 'begat' Comgall MacDomangart;

who in his turn begat – *aheugh!* – MacComgall,
begat Ferchar . . . begat Ainbcellach Mac

*cheugh!* Mac Ferchar, begat *aheugh!* Muiredach
Mac – heigh, ho – Eochaid the Venomous –

and thirty more I *could* name, but for this
*caaatchoo!* – down to your own John Smith. *Ahem.*'

# Fergus of Galloway

(Fergus attempts to make off with the shield of Dunottar)

When Fergus drew his pathetic weapon,
The dragon froze, with her mouth open –
As if to say, *I'm petrified*;
That the doomed knight might peep inside
Her filthy width of flame and froth –
Then shut it, with a snap of wrath.

No man in such a pass would choose
To linger with all he had to lose:
None but Sir Fergus, who possessed
The stoutest heart in the South West.
So there he stayed, at the beast's whim,
Until she slapped her tail at him,

Which made him glad he'd grabbed the shield;
For though it cracked, it wouldn't yield,
And kept him – for the moment – sound. –
But then he tried to stand his ground,
And found his boots were treading water,
And as he cartwheeled through Dunottar

He struck a wall with such a crack
His ribs were crushed against his back,
And all his senses so displaced
He thought he heard a burning taste.
The dragon, meanwhile, stopped and wept
At the cradleside where her shield had slept,

As if in a Highland melodrama.
Sir Fergus cursed through buggered armour.
His only solace where he lay,
That chevalier of Galloway,
Was joining, where he moaned and bled,
The ranks of the heroic dead.

For so much blood had spouted out
Of his wounds from the first blow of the bout
That when his eyes fell on the hue
Of the tunic he had put on blue,
He almost fainted in distress
At the ruined state of his warrior dress.

Instead, provoked by the red rag,
He sprang up, like a cornered stag,
And threw the weight of his wounded pride
At the tough scales of the lizard's hide –
Then slicing up at her peevish head,
Punctured the neck and dropped her dead.

Now, had you asked him to disown
His day's work, for the English throne
Or a long drink from our Saviour's Cup,
He would have told you to shut up,
So pleased was he to sniff the air
As Fergus of Galloway – Dragon-Slayer!

(from the French poem *Fergus*, c.1155)

# Wizard

Through the poor trees of Rhymer's Wood that was,
Merlin has run to his moulting cage, to moult:
'My God, my God, why hast thou forsaken me?'
– *Because because because because because!*

# Michael Scot

(1175–1232)

A fresco in the church of Santa Maria Novella
in Florence shows a friar urging repentance
on a crowd which seems to resent doing what it's told;

except in a bottom corner, where a singular blue figure
in a dunce's peaked cap and corset is
already ripping to pieces his banned book.

That one is Michael Scot of Peeblesshire:
who spurned his shepherd's birthright, and rode south
on a grey mare, after the star of knowledge:

to Oxford, where he bent the yew and the willow;
and Bamberg, a boom town, built on wizardry;
Toledo, where they forged his wand for him;

who pitched at last, astrologer at large,
into that crucible of the metric East
and Holy Rome that was Palermo then.

By day he would translate the secret books
of the Moor Averroes (who dared propose
sunlight between philosophy and God),

and went upstairs at night to play with fumes
and phosphor, and many a weird and future thing
hallooed from the pink mist of his magicking.

But when he once conjured himself, dead –
struck by a pebble, or mystery pellet – he quit
provoking heaven; took to the conical hat;

and broadcast those amends, by the despatch
in galley-chains of his appointed demon
to weave ropes of sand round the Bass Rock.

But the stone grew inwards. And the Florentine,
keeping a niche for everyone, has dropped
*Michele* without his brain in the Eighth circle,

among those seers, that for their forwardness
are trained to shuffle about with heads wrenched
back on their necks – rear-gunners, in hell-speak.

And worse: this shining, locomotive Scot
is strapped to the *Jimmie Mirror*, which lampoons
his magus as a slovenly patriot.

# Sweetheart

*On Founder's Day, Thursday, July 16, Mr Andrew Spottiswoode, owner of Sweetheart Abbey (at New Abbey in Dumfriesshire), played host to a meeting of Balliol's 'Sweet Sixteen', the Club reserved for the most distinguished of all our alumni, which meets, in its own rubric, every so often: on this occasion, as the centrepiece of that part of our septcentennial celebrations which extended 'beyond the Broad'. Drinks were served on the turfed nave of the old Cistercian abbey church, among the evening shadows cast by the masonry of the ruined building. There followed a brief service, conducted by the Master of Masters, and an address given by Mr Belloc. At an enjoyable dinner, given at the nearby Criffel Inn, where the company lodged for the night, members reminisced happily into the early hours. The guest speaker was the celebrated Rugby footballer Mr Richard Sharp, stand-off half in the Balliol and England XVs and fresh from his triumphs of the spring, who delighted most guests – if not the Snell Exhibitioner, Mr Smith (1740)! – with an account, entitled 'The Hammer of the Scots', of his well-kent deeds at Twickenham. The other members present were: the Cardinal Manning, with Gerard Manley Hopkins; Lords Curzon, Asquith, Ratcliff, Milner and Grey, with Lady Grey; Messrs Swinburne, Arnold and Gay; The Prime Minister, the Right Hon Mr Harold Macmillan; and Mr Edward Heath, MP. Mr Graham Greene sent his regrets.*

– Balliol College, Oxford, *Annual Record*, 1964


The hymn, 'Eternal Master, Strong to Save',
Loosened the rusted clamp of rigor mortis
And coughed old Jowett from the Balliol grave:

Amazing; clutching a can of breathing ether,
But unassisted; now in his hundred-and-forties,
More bird than man, more fossil coot than either;

Opening his Stoic or Silurian beak
In measured silence (nodding to Saint Paul),
To give the introit in an Ancient Greek.

Then upped the perpetual DUX with that poem again,
His party piece, beginning, 'Balliol made me . . .',
And ending, 'God be with you, Balliol men!'

Who further dared, that wine-blown son of Belial
Harp on an undergraduate anagram
Of his own handle, 'I CHEER BALLIOL!'

Trusting (his bullying term) that most of us
Would find these *jeux* amusing; 'given I am
Both funny hee-hee, and funny *Hilaire*-ious!'

This was bathetic. Self-regarding. Still,
The chorus bore him up with its usual will:
'*Floreat Domus. Dulce Cor. Amen.*' . . .

As if it were a wreath, they leant to lay
Their stone over the place by the high altar
Where Lady Devorgilla of Galloway

(Her family badge, two broken bones in saltire)
Was buried, with the embalmed heart beside her
Of John de Baliol, her immortal spouse

(The Baliol crest, a laughing skull and spider),
Whose penance for throwing stones at a bishop's house
Was founding with his confiscated dollars

A shelter, in a plain suburban villa
At Oxenford, for sixteen humble scholars,
Which had no roof, the day he died; until,

Granting the College arms and a coat of plaster,
With legendary love Devorgilla
Redeemed the flesh of her frail mate and master.

～

A floral bedroom, four in the bloody morning:
Belloc awake, cursing the human lot,
His mind a peewit, as an indigestive
Room-mate – 'Chesterton?' – got up in moonlit

Knickers and baby onions and string vest
To tiptoe from their bedside to the loo
delicate    delicate    delicate    – *fart*;
And then it seemed that *he* was walking, too,

Out from the Cloisters of the Tender Heart
With a cold wind flaming about his back
Across the fields; till, at a thundercrack
He fetched a shower of sparks from the victor's heel

As over the crown or brow of the Criffel Hill
There loped at him the leopard and furious Scot
To scorch those blond domains of Balliol
For Bruce, and Mary of the Expungèd Spot.

# Flower of Scotland

The arch-appeaser Balliol – dubbed a 'king'
By England's King (also, 'the little arse-licker') –
Whose two-faced father mined Dumfries, yet built
Oxford her nursery school – is history
The moment the Bruce appears from the priory, panting,
His sword in bloom, 'Comyn . . . the Red . . . is *killt*!'
(Comyn of Badenoch, a Balliol man),
And Bruce's boys pile in 'to mak siccar'.

So by their murderous pride they raised the flag
At Bannockburn, that fell in the mud at Flodden,
Where Scotland braved a general massacre
Of soldier, sovran, noble and downtrodden.
Woe was Dunbar, mourning his sick makars.
The Highland version lasted till Culloden.

# Wallflower

> . . . the name
> Of Wallace to be found, like a wild flower,
> All over his dear Country . . .
>     – WORDSWORTH

'In Vogue', but also in my garden:
    The scent of homegrown champion
Was out, between our moonlit beds
    And the rubble of white campion

(*Silene alba*; hairy perennial;
    Native wherever a cause is found;
Flowers from May to October;
    Favours disturbed ground).

We know how certain nights they cruise
    The length of the city wall, on foot,
In the Scotland strip, to court abuse
    Or pose for a photo-shoot;

But doubly strange, for me: to find
    The Wallace, first – then have to depict him,
Not as a freedom fighter, mind,
    But as a fashion victim!

For here, he was sporting a hose and sark
    In the 'Fairways' sett, of browns and mauves:
Not women's, but beyond the mark
    Where a man's clothing becomes clothes,

The country, town; with an overskin
    Of velvet, parted into four
Like the hockey shirt of the Harlequin:
    Azure and sable, gules and or

(A quarter gold, a quarter black,
    A quarter red, and a quarter blue),
And each with its buttoned hole in the back
    To tug one of his organs through,

The heart, the liver, lungs and spleen:
    Those relics to be borne away
To Haddington, and Aberdeen,
    To Galloway and Stornoway.

It seemed a rum choice of jacket
    For quite so fine a fugitive:
Chalked up, for anyone to hack at,
    Like the trace-coat of a Smithfield beef!

(I ought to add, that in a sling
    Bearing a bent spike for a bonnet,
He twirled his head, like a precious thing
    With the price still on it.)

Yet then he seemed to shudder, as all
    My eye was taken with his gear,
And in a grating whisper, told me
    News which even now I fear . . .

This done, the moon went overhead;
    The bell of Mary Magdalen
Struck one; and smartly off he sped
    In several directions.

# Guelf

Love moves the family, but hate
makes the better soldier;
why would the boxer scatter his purse,
sell up his soul, be Ugolino evermore,
for the soft-hard piece of his rival's ear –
were it not for the lovely taste of hate;
if it didn't award him a pleasant pillow
of hate to soften the stone of his cell?
*Dante, who loved well because he hated,*
*Hated the wickedness that hinders loving.*

# Braveheart

(1329)

THE SPRING: – and as her ice draws off the glen
Scotland gets up, and is herself again;
Hawthorn has run in white to the riverside
Where bluebells crowd the bank, and the young Clyde
Skips down the hill with a fresh appetite
On stones as clear as the stars on a frosty night;
The hedge-birds hop and sing; the lambs uplift
Their heads, and try their legs; the odd miffed
Hare kicks shadows, while a spider trails her new
Laborious lifeline down the lanes of dew,
And all the deads of winter pass away
In Mary's month, the miracle of May.

But not in the royal infirmary at Cardross,
Where Robert Bruce lies mortally leprous:
Mumbling instruction – as around him droop
The flowers of his barony in a hapless group –
That when they send his carcass to the crypt
The heart should be removed, embalmed and shipped
On the pilgrimage his cares had kept him from,
And get its burial in Jerusalem:
Either before the Holy Sepulchre,
Where Mary Magdalen found her gardener,
Or in the thistled plot by the Dragon Gate;
And so in a borrowed year to wipe the slate

Of old offence – and speed his soul to God.
The voice failed; and the barons' general nod
Settled its grave injunction on Sir James,

Douglas 'the Black', a known keeper of flames
(Badge of the Douglases, a burning bonnet
With an unburnt salamander sitting on it).
And when no further pulse of him was heard
They took their dead king at his dying word
And from its shell of ribbed and yellow bone
The rough, distended organ was withdrawn
And packed in a hand-grenade of Ailsa granite
For transit halfway over the known planet.

∼

THE NEXT SPRING: – and they gathered as decreed
Beside their boats at Berwick on the Tweed:
Sir William Keith, the Twa Lockharts of Lee,
And sixty more, sumptuous of pedigree,
Each with his *corps-des-armes* to man the deck;
And Douglas, with a heart around his neck.
Trimmed for the south, their sturdy fleet set sail,
Hauling its course through waterspout and whale,
Sea-wolves, and other monsters of the main,
Until they reached the sheltering coast of Spain
And climbed ashore, to fortify their will
Among the palms and fountains of Seville.

*Ay, freedom is a noble thing* . . . and these
Guid lairds have lent their men an evening's ease
To observe the local licence, and the sloth
That riots in the Sevillian undergrowth
Of tamarisk, wild figs and oleander;
So let us wink at Tam and Alexander
Crashing amongst the *vinos Andaluz*
To deaden the coming toll of Scottish youth;
Until the port bell chimes with the Angelus,

And someone snuffs a candle for the Bruce;
And soldiers fold, though morning vapours creep
About them, into nothingness and sleep.

Douglas said two words to his snoring men –
'Get up!' – and swept them to their oars again;
For while their morning-watch had blinked away
He'd had his breakfast with the teenage Rey
Of Gran Castile, Alfonso Love-the-Land,
Who'd shrewdly got 'the Black' to understand
That Osmyn the Orange, the five-hundred-acre
Lord of Granada, a Moorish troublemaker,
Had taken leave of his Arabian senses
And felled the uprights of their common fences
To extend his orange grove's perimeter
Beneath a crescent moon and scimitar.

Alfons, in a phrase that echoed through the heat,
Had vowed *to press these Moors beneath his feet*,
And urged his guests to play the white man's part
For all their urgent business of the heart.
Douglas lit up – a Christian leopard, he,
As ever he saw the cross in jeopardy –
Snatched at the chance to strike that heathen lord
With the sign of the Holy Rood and the broad sword,
And rowing his troops up a lethargic river,
The mazy, blockaged, rat-run Guadalquivir,
Disposed their arms, to toss his fortune's caber
In battle, near the burnt-out town of Teba.

Since here – in place of the proud Saracen
Of children's tales – a half-starved garrison
Peered from the gates, and on the summons made
Reluctant rows, like convicts on parade,

The Douglas, thinking the battle was in the bag,
Sounded his charge, and spurred his Solway nag
To bring it home; but on that foreign plain
The quivering mirage of the Moorish line
Ebbed and evaded his mounted men, who found
Their enemy had upped and quit his ground
Before they'd had a chance to kill him first;
And better judgment yielded to blood-thirst.

Alas for chivalry! This was the trick
Of feigned retreat, which, from the Arabic,
*El Cid*, at war a hundred years ago
With Moorish allies and a Moorish foe,
Had learned to keep a watch for; but the Scot,
Brought up on civil warfaring, had not.
Now both the observant chroniclers have said,
The Barbour and Le Bel, how Douglas read
Those buzzards round the sun as a fair sign
(The Douglas badge, described by Ballantyne
As 'a toad encyrcled by a flammand hat');
The Scots rode in pursuit, and that was that.

Wallop, and hiss, and fade. As waves break over
The Leith seawall, or froth the flags at Dover,
A tide of Moors swept round and through the force
Of dour, inflexible Scots and their spent horse.
Douglas, on his poor charger panicking,
Undid the pilgrim part of his late king,
Imploring, like a lamprey to the light,
'You, who were always first into the fight,
Our eager prefix, – *ay gannand afore* –
You get us out of this one, *Fortis Cor*!',
And wheeled his arm, and flung it, and before
It hit the ground the Douglas was no more,

But the shell burst. And what a heart it hatched!
Robert *Redux*, of nerve and muscle matched,
Who opened the pink gauze of his eyeflap
On vistas of olive toes and a sandalstrap
And shouted, – 'Get tae hell, ya Saracen git!
Mohammit gangs tae bed wi' a dummy tit!' –
Till seeing one Dervish pause in his footprints
To stamp his pound of offal into mince,
This remnant of our once and future Bruce
Set his survival skills to hyper-use:
Lay flat as fishies. Lay for a week, perhaps.
Then ached towards the north, trailing his pipes.

# Bell the Cat

(1483)

The cat was not called Bell, or Belle.
One day, when Scotland was unwell,

A clutch of Lowland noblemen
Met in a hall in Dunfermline

Seeking a means to dock the power
Of the sleek and sleekit Earl of Mar,

A bastard born as Robert Cochrane,
Pet of their incumbent sovereign.

Lord Gray, who sat at the head of the table,
Regaled his peers with the challenging fable

Of a timorous wee parliament of mice
And the big she-cat who bossed their house:

All were agreed that could they fix
A bell round the neck of their dominatrix,

They could be warned of her whereabouts
And scamper off with their cheese and sprouts;

But, being mice, they wouldn't do it.
Silence fell. Then, cutting through it,

A Douglas, with the Douglas wrath
Igniting through his beard of broth,

The red-faced Earl of Angus spat,
'I am he who will bell the cat.'

Three days, and Mar was rodent-fodder
Hung from the packman's bridge at Lauder.

# Selkirk

Fye upon yellow and yellow
  And fye upon yellow and green;
But up with the true blue and scarlet . . .
      – OLD SONG

It must have been a woman who wrote 'The Flowers
of the Forest' – meaning the Ettrick Forest, stripped
of its cover for spears and trench-props – not a man,
if after Flodden there were none left, saving
yon who sleepwalked home with his silly banner.
He rises every June at the Common Riding,
and when the trades lay down their flags, waves it
in semaphore, in silent figures of eight.

No wonder then, after Gallipoli,
the Selkirk Ladies dig in against all-comers;
or close around the Green, brilliant with menace,
where the strayed guest, be she a Gala Girl
in school maroon, or a Kelso bluestocking
hot from her tennis, a hem hoicked to the knee,
will catch the common greet of '*Luke Fifteen! –*'

*Bring forth the best robe, and put it on him; and put a ring on his hand,
and shoes on his feet: and bring hither the* fatted calf, *and let us eat, and
be merry: for this my son was dead, and is alive again; he was lost, and is
found.*

# The Queen's Maries

'*Old, old, old.* It's all you ever hear
when you get to be eighty-three and deaf as a post −'
so no bad thing if she's doing all the talking
alone in her café at Dumfries bus depot;

and plenty to shout about, given her cancer,
'Titania' knees, failed blood, and a spleen saved
for the ministers of the Solway Health Authority:
'Pardon my French, but if for whatever reason

you happen to wander a foot off their prescription
by smoking a matter of forty or fifty a day,
they want sod all to do with you' − so saying
she disappears in a pall of her own making.

'I'm soft in the head, and know it, and wouldn't
completely disown it − seeing the rewards, if less,
are different − days when your friend's about −
your lambswool blanket − *Crossroads* − coffee − Bingo!'

~

'What scares some people is losing their memories.
Fine, if you've got a particular story to tell,
but don't pretend they're gospel or gold coin,
mine anyway, mischief and rubbish, mostly.

My earliest one was always meant to be
this image of a train leaving a station,
the 'Highland Brownie', namely, bound for Oban
out of Queen Street: the heads of the city boys,

wedged at the windows, shorn for the day, trailing
their bits of streamer, smaller and brighter now,
as the cars pull round and away beyond the brick.
Only one morning my sister says to me,

you couldn't have watched the Brownie – we
were *on* it – and describes the seats for proof;
so *fup*! – there it goes again, the faulty wiring,
the tinnitus, the memory playing tricks.

– Think of the moors at evening, when the mist
rolls over everything: you keep your head,
as long as you stick to the fog in front of you,
don't poke for a path round, through, or under it.

And what if we don't have larks – we nurse instead
internal nightingales, their *clank*, *tweet*
a boiler slowing down; as the Firth fades
at sunset, and clouds are the last things lit.'

         ∾

'This famous picture, then. Glasgow again;
and Scottish, of course, but also Victorian,
and painted, they said, before they raffled it,
not from the life, but rather historical.

On one side was the Black Mass of Dumbarton;
on the other, the masts of a gallery, too big for the harbour,
fitted for Brest and the French prince or Dauphin;
and in between a stretch of cobbles, laid

to shine in the rain and light, with the glimmer of scales
in a fish-market; and every stone, they said,
had another great painting painted inside it,
in microscope – the Last Fish Supper or whatnot.

It made me proud, me being a Mary,
like taking the star role in Nativity,
how the whole scene revolved around her halo,
that red-head: already no better, we saw,

than we should be, a mischievous spark of six: –
and the extras were just her train, the two or three
miniature lairds and the other infant Marys,
the guilty, bearded men bugging the background.

And surely it's nature, to sweep things together
when we look back; for then it was always
the future, limitless, chancy, and no contradiction
between being Mary and also one of the crowd.'

∽

'Glasgow again, in nineteen forty-eight,
for Scotland–England: it's Solway grass, you know,
the sacred turf, the kissing turf; Hampden,
and Wembley too, came out of Cummertrees.

We were a hundred thousand, all of us Scots,
an army, like, but each his own commander;
we might have won, too, but for the goalie,
a lanky, unfortunate critter from Heart of Midlothian.

. . . By then it was over for us. He used to do
those French songs of the day, "Mimi", "Louise",
putting on his daft international accent;
it tickled me, all right: he was *my* Dauphin,

my own Chevalier. Him and his pals were part
of the Phibian Landings; not D-Day, but
a fortnight later – their pontoon was meant
to rebuild bridges behind the Canadians:

but the boat got shelled in the bay, he drowned,
they all drowned. And tell me if this is uncommon:
I loved him. I still love him, really. But then
I forget if he's Jackie or Hughie. – Here's the bus.'

～

Best and prettiest of Scottish names,
there are no new Marys anymore;
and this late flowering, after how many years
of making other peoples' beds in barracks,

hotels and hospices, got her modest send-off,
her jet brooch, bizzy lizzy and bus pass,
on the very day Mrs Thatcher decided
that any man over the age of twenty-six

who took the *bus*, could *count himself a failure*, –
whereas, she guessed, 'the clapped-out dames like us
were just coming into our own ("Excuse me, son,
these priory seats are reserved for me and my shopping!")'.

Thank heavens, likewise, for all the little girls
or not so little, ganging upstairs in a spiral
of swear words, text-tones, midriff and brutal candy
to back-seat country, putting as much distance

as buses allow between them and the elderly.
Some France they had: a dingy day out in a tunnel, –
but they tag on to the roll of great explorers:
'There was me, Shaneel, Shell and Michelle –'

# Knox

INQUISITOR:                    . . . When did
   You last see your father or beat your wife?
CONFESSOR: My wife and I are unmarried, – and I beat the lady,
   Within an inch or two of my own life.
      – OLD PLAY


Because, though the beard was just beginning,
the captives called him Chaplain; because he looked
thistles the whole time, and full of righteous
hate in the Scots tradition – he stuck out,
even among the rowers' rows of the galley;
so the French crew would bait him. One, at Brest,
approached him with a petite carving of
Their Lady (School of Avignon, boxwood,
early sixteenth century), made him hold Her,
and wondered in menacing terms whether
the Chaplain might not like to kiss Her toes;
at which John Knox, *no whit emasculate*,
shouted out hoarsely that this *She* was *bot*
(I write the words as he would see them printed)
*a peynted brodd*, and flung it overboard –
and before they could lay their hands on him, got off
another half-jet of disdain, that the piece
being wooden was fitter for swimming than worsh—

        ∾

*The name 'poppy-head' refers to the carved finial, used to complete the
top of the bench end and peculiarly English in character. It had been per-
fected by the close of the fifteenth century, and was then in regular use for
benches of the nave as well as in the choir. The relatively simple fleur-de-
lys form of poppy-head, suitable for the village, is seen to perfection in the
ladies' pew at Trunch, Norfolk, and the very elaborate form, where the*

[33]

*poppy-head springs from a crocketed circle filled in with sculpture, at St Nicholas, King's Lynn. . . . Occasionally the convention was departed from and the finial carved like a lemon or diamond. The side of the bench, meanwhile, might be enriched with elaborate tracery or domestic scenes, or might consist of a mass of sculpture in perspective, with canopy work, buttresses and sculptured niches. . . . Some beautiful stall ends are seen at the Louvre: a tree is sculpted as growing from the mouth of a dragon; another is seen to emerge from the mouth of a fool.*

～

The bit where they clapped him, sarcastically, into
their dungeon, and slammed him in – that might have hurt
another man; or seemed like passing down
to the latter world – seeing he missed his footing and went
over the side of a set of steps, landing with two
bangs on his hip and elbow, suddenly lying
winded, and who knows where, in the pure dark.
No light from any window; none from under
that door he'd fallen from. But being young,
and bearing the tonic of fight around as part
of his person, he drew there on the trick his elder
sister had told him once, in a Lothian close,
against night blindness, shutting the eyes tight
for say ten seconds; so, when he faced them again,
the walls of the room were blank, but visible.
As a space for sleep and prayer it was serviceable.
This was the minute (he would tell us later),
within that cell at sea, or the hold of France,
that first unveiled for him the lineaments –
only the planes of bench seating to add, and
nothing more privy or plush for its minister –
of 'John's', the standard, disembellished Kirk.

# Inkhorn

*Il n'importe rien* – for export only

My part? – reciting the Seven Ages of Man,
with not enough *gusto,* apparently,
in an orange wig, while all around me rolls
'Time's Whirligig' – the Brownies doing cartwheels
over the forestage and the apron stage.

(If last year's show was a modest hit – 'Winston
at the Church Hall': I sang the Cliffs of Dover,
and the rest evolved from the sketches Geoff had kept
in mothballs from his salad days with ENSA
– the chemistry's not there with *Gloriana*.)

To help us round what Geoffrey calls
a little 'local difficulty', he proposes
that where in the final line the writer uses
French, 'sans eyes, sans teeth' (though pardon me,
dentures – didn't the Queen have a wooden set?),

we substitute *without* in each case, that way
it won't seem 'callous or condescending' (in my view,
should mine be wanted, the English softens the force).
They're charging five pounds to get in, but for
that you are also entitled to a buffet supper.

– Geoffrey, who would style himself Sir Walter,
and stars in a silent tableau of that knight
strolling along the prom at El Dorado
with a pipe and a baked potato, his tights worn
*under* a patent 'Hammond' or cricket box,

will swear – though he must be eighty, now – he once
saw a film called *Finish Your Bowls!*, in which
it was either Dietrich or Mae West – halted
on the half-landing and said, 'I may look like
a lady, but these are the bosoms of a *bitch*.'

The *Pict* no shelter now shall find
Within his party-coloured mind;
   But from this Valour sad
   Shrink underneath the plaid;

Happy if in the tufted brake
The English Hunter him mistake,
   Nor lay his Hounds in near
   The Caledonian Deer.
      – MARVELL, 'An Horatian Ode upon Cromwell's Return'

# The Honours

When James the Sixth went South, to be the First,
He abandoned the honours of Scotland, her national regalia,
The crown, the sword of state, and the Sceptre of Judah,
Those durable symbols of Scottish success or failure,
   And died in his absence of the bloody flux.

And when his son let both their realms riot
In lawlessness and civil war, resistance
Whisked the three treasures out of the capital,
North to Dunottar, for their safer keeping,
   As evening herdsmen fold away their flocks:

And when a siege was laid by that cruel fox
Commander Lambert, known as 'Cromwell's Cunt',
A patriot at a venture, a Mrs Granger –
Wife of their minister, praying the while
   *The Lord is my Shepherd, I shall not want* –

Begged her admission through the Castle gate
To relieve a distressed mother within of the worst
Of her feminine waste: so under the English nose
She smuggled the sceptre, the crown and the sword of state
   Out in a wagon of dirty clothes and (she said) flax.

[37]

# Embedded

Our Hero, a some-day painter, obtaining a pass through Time
courtesy of Scotrail and Nelson's Red Series of portable classics
for a touch of the Highland lowlife, the smoke on his heather, is
    waking
up with a terrible start – far from himself, – from two hours'
    sleep

*oh, God* – and a whisky duel with the elder MacAulay, the same
ambiguous host who is now driving their cattle over the foot
and head of his bed-space, over the actual cloth of his
pillowcase – and seizes a moment – before, he imagines,

one of their Morags will stick him under the ribs with a coarse
or comical thrust, just to get hands on a pencil sketch
of 'Loch Awe by Moonlight' and muff it away in her hairy
    clothing
– a moment to jot on the card backing his sketchbook,

'God help the prospector who comes to these people with hopes
of promoting the Union; they may be surrounded
by dramatic mountain scenery, but they set little enough
store by the values of peace and quiet, *ditto* prosperity.'

# Maroon

(1703)

It's just as well the man of Fife is neither
hostage to fancy, nor socially over-particular.
Before he is half-dry, he has put behind him
the rough justice you get as a sailor, and won't dwell
long on the rights and wrongs of his own case:

whether, in the Captain's terms, his Mate
was a bugger; or the Captain a thief, scanting
an honest Scot and his fellow mariner
of the spoil-share due to a crew member . . .
Indeed, it is only by seconds his second thought

when the *Mungo* pulls from the bay
that there's still plenty left of the day,
and since he unquestionably is marooned –
four hundred to the west of Valpareez –
he might as well settle to whittle the staves

of his new place: a basic shelter first,
until in time a house of logs should crown
all these unlikely acres. Looking up,
where a green cleft in the rock-face marks
his freshest water, berries that will be.

So, not for him the harrowing detailed once
on the next island, by a Dutch counterpart,
whose every prayer for a sheet or sail was fouled
by invisible spirits, hissing his offence at him
from behind boulders, or out of caverns. – No,

when the seals give up their morning holler
and slip into the warm pacific, there remains
to the civilised ear, no sound but the shush
of wind in God's pimentos, or the light scree-shift
of high goats making themselves innocent.

There on the damp walls
    Of your ancestorals
Rust hath corrupted the armour of Albin.
    Seize, then, ye madd'ning Macs,
    Buckler and battle-ax,
Lads of Lochaber, Breadalbane, Clan-Alpin!
    – OLD SONG

## The Lost Leader

In which a fly
Pilots a dry
Course through rain
And back again.

*And Micaiah said . . . I saw all Israel scattered upon the hills, as sheep that
have not a shepherd: and the Lord said, These have no master: let them
return every man to his house in peace.*

∾

At Ruthven, by Spey ford,
It poured all day, around
The blown-up barracks, while we
Waited on your permission –
Sixteen hundred far-gone
Followers to the bone –
Until, at dusk, your plump
Liveried aide-de-camp
Wound up the slope
    On a yellow mare:

Who took as long as it took
To deposit, instead of an order,
*Let each seek his own safety*
*The best way he can –*
And down the hill again,
In coats of soaking silk.
We only had to weigh
That foreign sentiment,
That *sauve qui peut.*
     If we'd wanted to save ourselves . . .

Royal of him, as well,
That with that fleeting gesture
He sent a verse of Scripture,
A screed from Jeremiah:
*Weep ye not for the dead,*
*Neither bemoan them:*
*but weep sore for him that goeth*
*away: for he shall return no more,*
*nor see his native country.*
     – So how could he leave it?

That night I entertained
Shadows the weak lamp
Threw on the grey-green
Walls of the world:
A body that twisted,
Grew, and shrank.
Wind was the only sound,
With the rain in it
And once a dismal scrowl
     Of wild cats, mating or fighting.

The fire of belonging was out.
I saw my way, sticking
The course of the Tromie,
Up to a poor shift made
Between rain and wood,
And yours: west down channels
Of last-ditch loyalty;
To France at last, your safety,
Prince, Your Highness,
     Your brandy, gout and syphilis.

～

*The cause was light,*
*A flower worn in the heart,*
*The secret white of the rose:*
*And all we did was sweetened by it.*

# Gray's Elegy

(1751)

> Alas for this gray shadow, once a man
> – TENNYSON

Always that bit of him seemed somewhere else,
As if he'd come not from 'Two-bloody-A'
And *Cider with Rosie*, but from table-talk
With Lamb and Hazlitt; we guessed he was gay.

One time we wondered, 'What does it mean, the title,
Far from the *Madding* Crowd? Are the crowd mad,
Or are they making the other person mad,
So he's had to run away? Is he in hospital?'

'Fair question; but the man you'd have to ask
Is Thomas Gray' – and all the sharper boys
Pounced on the slip – 'You mean, Thomas *Hardy*',
And mocked him with a gentle *durring* noise.

'No, no, I don't. You see, while Hardy *chose*
His title, it was then the common course
When giving a book a name, to plagiarize
An apt quotation from another source.

'As those who did "Fitzgerald and his World"
Will know, the title *Tender is the Night*
Derives from Keats; it wasn't Hemingway
For whom the bell tolled in the copyright;

'And *Far from the Madding Crowd* is commandeered
From a very famous poem by *Thomas Gray* –
Gray's Elegy, is how it's known – which starts,
"The curfew tolls the knell of parting day . . ."'

[44]

He brightened briefly – 'Say we read it through –
To find what other lines this poem has lent!'
But there were no Grays left in the stock room,
So we talked about Hardy's wives till the bell went.

# Herries

(1753)

Through some rough *droit*, embedded in his shield
Of *argent trois urcheons sable* – in British,
Three black hedgehogs crossing a silver field
But slowly, so they pass for dead or dormant –

He gets to plant his boots under our table.
Feeds absently – wrapped in a cause beyond
Our country codes and kinship; doesn't care
Whose bearing makes his host uncomfortable.

Will prick at his orange till the juice runs out;
Or when Father, gamely proposing 'the King',
Forbears to press the name of George, will pass
– You watch! – his cup *over the water*-jug,

While two free fingers scissor or walk in air
Like Christ's white legs skimming the German Sea.

# Not Jenny

To Chatham, where the great military mastodon
Musters to crush a distant colonial insect.
The King is hosting dinner. And through its hours and courses,
Its sculpted fats and fishes, eggs and roe,
Beauty-spots bob like shot in the eye.

Sunset. The port sways in candlelight; a steady
Slipping away, through narrow doors and passages,
Of men with order sheets, others with women or bottles.
The next day, the King might leave. Or stay.
For now, he gets in stages to his feet, to launch

On a speech which fails to deliver its trivial story –
How his mistress Jenny (now nudging his knee-bone)
Neglected to curb a pet gooze, a black gooze
That had fallen him    followed him    through the ways
Of a maze and it bitten him on the

– She has to join to steer him on, their voices
Clashing – 'His *Rear End*' – 'my be-behind!'
Till the joke wears audibly thin, and the King
Aborts to the toast, 'Not Jenny'. 'The *anti*-toast,
NOT JENNY', again, repeated till none take it up.

At which he has lost himself. Others, maybe,
Are wilder or worse, but there goes the King –
As if elsewhere, on the eve of scarlet adventure,
Up an unguarded inlet, a smeared nocturnal agent
Had snipped our row-boat from its reedy mooring.

# Proscription

Like the Children of Israel
in bondage to the King of Egypt,
  we have so little standing:
  they call us only 'Jock'.
    – IAN LOM, 'A Lament for the State of the Country'

On Friday last, by Cripplegate, I was overhauling
a Jew's wallet, in quest of certain vestments through a collection
which I was assured were *verrrry new* – when a stranger

whose latter end plainly demonstrated the nature of his errand
crossed the alley, and in the broadest Scotch I think I'd ever
    heard,
accosted the Israelite, 'Hae ye got onie breeks i' your bag?'

Struck with the oddity of his address, and the well-known
    dialect
of my native country, I looked steadfastly at the man,
and in his features thought I observed remote tints or lights

of a dream I had, ten, twenty years ago – such is the savour
of old acquaintance. A moment more – 'Gude Life!' said I,
'It couldna be – Y'are nae *MacGregor*, man? – . . . Oops!'

. . . Two traders reminisce. 'Ah, Cairo . . . what about M'ahmet
    Begg,
with that green turban o' his? – We played him a trick once –
    poured
a whole pint o' brandy into his sherbet! – Now, the old rogue
    takes care

he doesna discover the ruse till he's supped to the moon o' the
   flagon,
and then he pauses, strokes his long white silky beard, and says,
I swear it, – *"Allah Kerim"* – you know, "Heaven is merciful"!'

# The Ayrshire Orpheus

And down he went, sounding the deepest floors
Where Pluto ruled with serious Proserpine,
Still piping, till he reached their double doors
And knocked. And so he saw her, horribly thin:
Eurydice, her face all eaten in,
Curled at the feet of that disdainful pair
Who feigned surprise to see a Scotsman there.

Then Orpheus, soft and urgent, half in dread
Of what she had become: 'My bonny lass –
Hey – love – though it's better than being dead –
What's happened to your lovely lips and face?
How have they disappeared, or come to this?'
And she: 'Shoosh, pet, right now I dare not say –
But you shall hear the whole another day',

As Pluto intervened: 'Your silly wife
Has marred her face, and turned her belly barren,
Through dwelling on the home she may not have;
Mindful of Ballantrae and the view of Arran,
She finds the mills of Hell friendless and foreign;
If one could spring her now to the Ayrshire coast,
No doubt her looks would heal to their uttermost!'

So Orpheus sat before that mocking twosome
And let them have it, with his matchless voice,
Pitching 'Ye Banks and Braes' at the royal bosom;
A charming 'Ae Fond Kiss', and 'Ca' the Yowes',
And then 'My love is like a red, red rose';
Till Pluto swooned, and prickly Proserpine
Lay down her softening form upon the green.

The infernal lakes had filled with lily water,
Such was the gentle power of that recital,
When Pluto cleared his throat: 'I thank the Scot
Who wrote these songs, and you, who made them vital;
Name your own prize, and that shall be requital.'
And Orpheus begged, 'Then let me take my love
Back to that place we owned in the world above.'

Which tickled Pluto. – 'You're a bold one, Mac!
– Yet I'm inclined to grant such a request,
On this condition: should you once *look back*,
Your wife reverts to Hell of the heaviest!'
Then Orpheus clasped her freshening to his chest,
And up they strove, spiralling in their fate,
Till they had almost reached the outward gate.

If you have loved, imagine the sweet chat
The two then had, rejoining their own kind –
So can you blame him, in the midst of that,
If he should suffer a local lapse of mind?
I hate to say – she fell a yard behind –
Backward he blinked – chains belted from the deeps
And yanked Eurydice to Hell for keeps.

Poor Orpheus! He felt like some old town
Of Carrick in decline: Maybole, or Girvan,
The pubs shut down, the kids, taunting 'the clown
Who couldna face the front', on drugs from Irvine;
While dismal in the twilight of surviving
Alone with his shopping, sore to be rid of her,
He walks the roads of home a widower.

# Elegy for the Greys

She knows this turf from Agincourt to Zutphen,
And pounces, when I air my prejudice
In favour of the Greys at Waterloo
(Heroes, who when they'd run their targets through
Galloped on over the hill for the joy or the hell of it):
'Put simply, it was crass indiscipline –

And cost the Duke his sole offensive arm.
Besides, the Inniskillings and the Royals
Were no less forward in that rush of blood;
The Blues, too, got an eagle, and they kept it!'
– She means it; so I don't object, *Your Blues*
*Did not ride navy horses; and they weren't Scots.*

&#126;

Chancing on courage and its clear mystery –
As if they'd glimpsed their future, in a hat,
Raking the field for loot, Belgian at best,
And seeing how a regimental suicide
Could scatter that – propelled them with a wink
Over the brink, bearskinned, immense, brazen.

Surely the giant sergeant, John McEwan –
'The Ajax of the Greys', his favourite Star
Doused in the mud, lolling her tongue, the long
Mechanical lancers fastening for the kill: –
Surely his mind, vaulting its circumstance,
Repairs in half-light up the Brussels road

Two nights ago, and stables off the *Place*,
And climbs a staircase to the Richmonds' ball
Before the word from Quatre Bras: that waltz;
Lifts of desire; Amelia's pregnant look;
The breeze of tittering after an old boy's boom
Echoed from wall to wall to chandelier?

# Diehard

(1832)

The young Scott, on a short lease at Lasswade,
Before he flit from poetry into prose,
Had tried his hand at breeding bantams – kinds

Of domestic fowl 'in which the cock is pugnacious'.
Only, through overbreeding, certain strains –
The Leinster Buff, with its tremendous neck

And breast, or the Scotch Grey – had grown effete,
And shunning a proud tradition, would rather flap
In circles round each other like big dusters.

Now Walter, whose own career in arms was curbed
In the right leg, by childhood polio,
Was game enough if a goose needed a boot;

And when the east coast flared with false alarm
Of a French landing, he formed with city friends
A legal militia, the Edinburgh Light Horse:

Saw action twice, helping to face down
Miners and mill-workers, but wore year round
Its scarlet uniform with sky-blue britches.

The Horse would laugh behind him, whether he led
Their exercise through Bonnyrigg, or growled,
Dismounting, at 'that infantry', their bairns;

While neighbouring farmers, though they loved no less
His songs and savoury stories, came to poke
Fun at the straighter face of the poultryman,

And when he lost a dozen birds to a fox,
Though all that time his run had been secure
'With wire intact to a height of three foot six' –

Gravely surmised, 'That maun be a *flying* fox';
'That, or maybe some gamefu' speerit has clapt
A pair o' wings on one o' your wee dugs!'

~

'*Testudo*' – as he signed one book review,
Alluding to the mode of the Tenth Legion
In Tacitus, of storming British positions

Beneath their shields, 'under a shield ceiling' –
Put up his nick-names, pen-names, *noms de guerre*,
'Shirra', 'My Landlord', 'Author of *Waverley*',

'The Wizard of the North', 'The Great Unknown',
And 'Laird of Abbotsford', as a plate of shields
From his mind's Melrose antique shop; as the means

Both to buy into and to dress the beams
Of that prose palace, his hobby and hungry folly.
And you might say, the Tweed's been up for grabs

Since tons of her softer, southern bank were forfeit
To Scott and a gas-lit Gothic anomaly. And yet:
When the capital comes, in golf-carts and garages

Rubbishing over the Abbotsford policies,
If the ghosts of Borders Past have kept a twelfth
Of the powers he assigned them in his *Minstrelsy,*

They'll yank the developers' feet from their four-by-fours
And shake them, till all the greed has chunkled
Out of the trouser bottoms – *yea, to the smallest change.*

For didn't he mind the crackpot and awkward acre,
Being, to hazard a swipe with a rusty phraser,
If not a *Nature's laird* then *bountiful maker*?

Look how he peopled the fields, they light up
When you say their names, *Dalgetty*, *Jarvie!*,
Not living, so much, as thoroughly acting the part,

With portable speeches and full stage-colouring:
Martyr and Highlander; lost children, heirs
To great estates; gypsies: Prince *and* Pretender.

The Scott novel's a 'Big Bow-Wow', shaggy,
Heavy, particular; slow to rouse; but once fixed,
Will not give up its grip on your reading leg.

                ≈

A son of the Manse, the painter David Wilkie
Would loiter in village fairs, or market places,
To execute in his Fife vernacular

The 'pauper style', learned from the Flemish (see
*The Cottage Toilet*, now in the Wallace Collection),
And so won youthful fame as the 'Scottish Teniers'.

In 1818, when our hero was offered,
And proudly accepted, the rank of Baronet,
Wilkie came over to paint a cabinet picture

Of Walter, his wife and weans as Border rustics:
Contrived by the painter this, by way of a break
From a weighty commission, *The Chelsea Pensioners*

*Receiving the London Gazette Extraordinary*
*Of June the Twenty-Second, 1815,*
*Announcing the Battle of Waterloo,*

For which the Duke of Wellington had advanced
Twelve hundred guineas – then a fantastic sum –
And that, they said at the *Heckler*, was just for the title.

(The kiss of death for Wilkie, a little later,
Was being appointed Royal Limner of Scotland:
For which there was no help but to depict

*The Entry of George the Fourth, in Highland Dress
To Holyrood House*, and render as rugged knee
The fat hock of Hanover; it wore the weeds

Of another formidable earner, but took him for ever,
Ate at his mind, fettered and followed him round
And turned out 'a horrible mixture of oil and water'.)

   ~

If Wilkie's star declined with the rise of Turner's,
The crash of Constable's washed Scott's, alas,
Unstable fortune in sheer lumps downriver.

   ~

For a few days, they say, he 'kept a face
Like thunder' – clicked his thumb ominously
At a black dog; but Scott would not go under.

One morning, he broke off the staring match
With bankruptcy – exclaimed to the family
'No! This right hand shall work it all off!'

Got up and (this was his finest hour) took seven
Even steps across the boards to his study, closing
The door behind him; just as if he meant

To collar the foam-jawed Beast of Debt in there
And tame her, with tickly, infinite strokes of his quill.
And truly, he wrote as long as he was able –

Not of his best – that went with the weathervane –
But colder things, to blunt the bills of ransom,
Napoleons, Demonologies, formula novels,

A difference lost on his detractors. 'Who now
Reads *Anne of Geierstein*?' Leavis would ask,
Deliberately choosing one of the least attractive,

As if his own tracts, while not exactly Gospel,
Or Acts, were forceful appendices tucked on these
– A tail. But who now reads *Revaluation*?

～

We won't look away at the end. – You found
Reform, woo-wooing down the lanes
Of Hawick and Jedburgh, anathema,

And it snapped back at you. After the fourth
Aggressive palsy, your 'sagacious' face
Frozen beneath its shaven skull and skull-cap,

You speak less, and less well. You don't see
That both your boys fall in behind you, soon,
And childless, and the hard-bought title with them;

That the passage will turn out rougher, not moonlit
As you might have told it: trepanned, stupid
With opium, howl, howling for all that . . .

So while you can, Sir Walter, father-figure,
Stay with your stalwarts in a shaded room:
The silent deerhound, Maida; then a pair

Of that box-nosed terrier, known in the kennel
As aberdeens, but called by the Borderer
'Diehard', for their tenacity in the field,

Which might endear them to an ailing master.
That way, like Dandie Dinmont in *Guy Mannering*,
You come to lend your name to a whole breed.

> The Hermit, . . . placing before the Saracen a pitcher of sherbert,
> assigned to the Scot a flask of wine
> – *The Talisman*

## John Imlah

'The Baird o' Bon Accord'

He never left his native Aberdeen,
*Where the triple rivers rin, sae clear and fresh*;
But since he bore the alcoholic gene,
Better if he'd been born in Marrakesh.

# Namely

'Angus Calder': it might have been piped by the Black Watch
or lowed by the Tweed; or plucked from the psalter of
    Hamish Imlach
(a singer so dyed in the cause, he was finally certified Scotch:
though less of a difference divides us than separates sameish
    and similar
– and besides, it was him, not me, they raised in the groves of
    Shimla,
while 'Sonny's Dream', his greatest hit, was Nova Scotian) –
but I've got this mongrel and seeming-Islamical M. IMLAH,
the SMITH, J. of phonebooks from Fez to the Indian Ocean.

For which I protest, there's a primary school near Edinburgh
that part of me never left, and cite my classmate Lorna
    MacDougall,
who grew up to share the name of the novelist Ishiguro,
'Ish' to his friends on the circuit, or point to the passage in
    Google
which proves IMLACH was what my family too had originally
    been,
Gaelic for *those of the loch*, until with the Clearance of Jura
the 'c' was lured from its croft by the trawlers of Aberdeen
and struck out o'er the moor, O.

[61]

So we've declined to this! – a prophet in black-face, fellow
to all those souls who have taken the bait of the Englisher
    Ashmole:
I wanted to play Macbeth, and they tricked me out as Othello
(*Makbeth*, in the Hebrew, is 'hammer'; *o' tellah*, in Farsi,
    'fishmeal').
And while my term is served, in a place off Portobello,
the woman who does my laundry unwittingly takes the
    Michael
by printing each week on the counterfoil for my wash-and-dry
    cycle
I, S, H  .  .  . – I'll have to tell her. 'Don't call me Ishmael!!'

*And the King of Israel said unto Jehoshapat, There is yet one man,
Micaiah the son of Imlah, by whom we may inquire of the Lord: but I
hate him; for he doth not prophesy good concerning me, but evil. And
Jehoshapat said, Let not the king say so.*

# Mary Queen of Scots

When trains had names: like 'Mary Queen of Scots',
A train which couldn't speak, but overheard
Nonsense of first-class passengers especially,
Who coming on at Waverley or at York
Were the closest to her engine and its ears;
Like Charlotte's nonsense, sprayed at the governess,
'Grace, I always thought Queen Mary was
An English Queen!' (*I always thought the Queen
Of England was a virgin – well, I'm not.*)

'Charlie', the late Countess of Wemyss (pronounced
*Weems*) was known to recount before friends
That when she was a little girl, returning
From the family August at their house in Fife,
She found herself, armoured with innocence,
Chosen above all children to bear witness . . .
How late into the afternoon, they changed
Trains for the Sussex coast: and Charlotte cried,
And pulled her bear; slept afterwards; and woke
With a taste for gingerbread, seeing a cottage
Completely covered in ivy, a happy straggle
Of farmers' children waving their stones and spears . . .
Westwards from Arundel was pastureland,
Browsing with cows, the river looping by,
Obscured by banks of gorse, thistle, and flint,
And specked with poppies; till the sights gave out
Like the lemonade. A second sulk came on,
At Chichester; and Gracie the governess,
Herself fed up by now, said 'Look, darling –
There's the cathedral!', and Charlotte, leaning out,

Surprised the arrogant ancient spire in the act
Of crashing down; and thinking little of it
Hated the babyish awe her nurse pretended.

That evening in the sidings at Kings Cross
The sleek Queen Mary had her private grouse,
Then shared it with a sleeping 'Joan of Arc':
'But if they had to wander back in time,
Let's say to mine – what difference would they find,
Expecting ruff and hose, and minstrels bright;
And what would smack them in the general face –
A great big smell of it – the draught that caused
Poor Charlotte in her mysteries to bawl out
"It just felt alien, Mummy!" – call it smell;
Composed of gunpowder, incense as well,
Dancing and sweat as well – You know the stuff
I mean, Joan; the "English" word was faith.'

# Railway Children

After the branch line went to Ochiltree –
I would have been fifteen – two men were shut
In the station waiting-room, and one of them
Brought out his pocket anecdote of me:

'The boy's a splurger! – hey, when Danny Craig
Passed him a flask on the train the other day,
He gulped it, just for the sake of showing off.
And he's a coward too, for all his face.
For after he'd taken the drink, he noised about,
And Dan, to clip his wings, made up a threat
To hang him out o' the window by his heels –
You know Dan didn't mean it, but the boy
Grew white at the very idea o't – shook
Like a dug in the wet – "*Oh!*," he cried, and "*Oh!* –
But how would tha ground go flying past your eyes;
How quick tha wheel beside your face would buzz –
Would blind you by quickness – how tha grey slag
Would *flash* below ye!" – Those were his actual words;
He seemed to see it all as if for real,
And flinched, and stopped, and stared, like a body in fits,
Till Dan was drawn to give him another drink;
"You'd spew with dizziness," he said, shut
His eyes where he sat, and actually bocked himself.'

## Precious Little

By the shore of Lake Constance I sat down and prayed
That your health should not collapse in an African swamp.
I found the name you carved before I was born
On the Tower of Pisa, and chiselled mine beneath it.
When our hotel in Brussels burned to the ground,
I fled with nothing but my bullfinch and your portrait, dear.

Two dreams: that you have come home at last
With your throat slit, and walk past me without speaking;
Or, as I roam the poor quarters of Mecca or Medina
In my loose nightgown, exhausted with yearning,
I cry aloud, 'Does he care for me?' –
And think I hear an angel whisper, 'Yes'.

# Begging

The job was, to eradicate deception
Amongst the beggars of the city: those
In earnest were entitled to their licence,
While cheats were to be cautioned, with a beating
Or a week in gaol, as they preferred, or both.

Me, I was clueless; till they teamed me up
With Dalton Bright, the 'Lambeth Labrador'.
Our first night out together, we found two
On crutches by the gates of Waterloo,
Boards round their neck like labels on decanters,

Declaring them A SAILOR OF THE FLEET
And SOLDEIR OF THE QUEEN. As we approached,
Dalton with real disgust said, '*He* a sailor?
Did you see him spit? He spat to windward.
A sailor would never spit to windward. Why,

He could not!' So the interview began:
What ship, what cargo, where . . . 'The Baltic, eh?!
Did you ever drink in the "British Flag" at Kiel?
What was the landlord's name? Was it not *Greaves*?
– You think so? – It was Baker. Leave your crutches.'

(And with a whipped seat stinging in his britches,
The sailor ran off with his legs.) 'And you, sir –
India – height of the Mutiny? Mmm, I guessed it
From the standard of your breath – which regiment
Was it you graced? Och aye! The Twenty-Third! –

*The Lord's my Shepherd*, Scotland forever, eh? –
You brazen impostor! The Twenty-Threes
Are the Royal Welch, and they did not go east
Till the June of Sixty-Five. I hate your sort!
Stand straight. Take off your hat. And beg directly.'

# The Four Marys of Melrose

(Rugby song)

The four Marys of Melrose:
Not all of them were Mary;
For one was milky Mary-Gwen,
Who splashed it about the dairy;
Marion let her butt and ben
Down by the Dean of Fairy;
While Mercy kept the grasses green
At the Abbey and cemetery.
The four Marys of Melrose:
And one of them was Magdalen.

# Rosebery

(Archibald Primrose, 1847– )

I'm not suggesting he was Oscar Wilde,
if I say, we all quoted him; he spoke
more squarely than that gentleman; besides,
his phrases had the stamp of mass production
and general currency – see, you probably
had one or two of them loose in your pocket:
*nation of amateurs*, *ploughing his furrow alone.*
And then his name, like Wallace or Wellington's,
crept into our streets and public houses:
he was the Earl of Rosebery, richest man
in Scotland; and, for an exacting year
and more, Prime Minister of the United
Kingdom of Great Britain and Ireland.

But there was one remark attributed
to Rosebery that I never liked (though why,
I wouldn't know till I was older), passed
at Parkhead, 1900: to the captain
of the Scottish eleven, which, taking the field
in Rosebery's racing colours of pink
and yellow hoops – he was their President,
but still, this seemed an honour overdone
to one not royal, exactly – had just thrashed
their English counterparts, four goals to one,
the greatest margin yet in the auld fixture –
holding his smile for the photographer –
'I haven't seen my colours so well sported
since Ladas won the Derby!' – *general laughter.*
(He'd left his Oxford college, not under

the usual cloud, but in a lord's dudgeon,
because the University rules required him
as an undergraduate, not to own a racehorse:
becoming an earl at twenty, he had said,
does not dispose 'one' to obedience.)
My thoughts were, then, that men should not be seen
in either of those two colours, or so nakedly
be made to run the race for someone else;
today, that he took one turf for another,
ours for his, and none had dared correct him.

Well, I had plenty to go on. My editor,
who'd used his club before the war, had warned me,
not disapprovingly, he could be cutting
and sarcastic: of his own wife, for instance,
as they left separately for a summer on Skye,
*Hannah and the rest of the heavy baggage*
*will follow later*; nor did he much enjoy
critical noises. But publicly he floated
on a cloud of pride, that bore him high and clear
like a balloon, whenever someone not
his equal – and surely few seemed otherwise –
appeared to him to be provoking him.

(At which he would lean back, hearing all this
quietly, only inflating slightly, as if to say,
'These' – quoting another – 'are certainly some
of my characteristics, and I glory in them.')

Known as unwounded, too – superbly so –
by innuendo, likewise implication,
he was forced (or so it seemed) to defend himself
in the skirmishes after the Queensberry hearing,
when rumours grew particular about himself

and the Marquess's son, and the blows got low
at the same time, round Rosebery's late wife.
Namely, as one of them dared in fact to put it,
'Why, sir, did you marry a Rothschild?' (meaning,
and understood to mean – *and one so plain
you can't pretend the attraction was natural*).
At which he glared for a moment at the questioner –
his eyebrows preternaturally still – and *quipped*,
would you believe, in the face of such ill-will,
'That we might lie together in life's index.'
Cool; pretentious; shutting them up for as long
as it took their wits to work it out; disdaining
to feed their envy. Then, '– Also, of course,
to get my greasy hands on the Mentmore stud.'

These were the means by which he kept warm
his authority, even when he was ailing.
At the hour of Armistice, which came, alas,
after his stroke – it rendered him speechless
into the autumn – and so failed to inspire him,
the whole host of Edinburgh gathered outside
his town house there, while he was propped upstairs
just semi-conscious – shouting out his name
like a football chant, *Rozbury, Rozbury,*
as if he'd scored twice on their piece of field.
And I suppose we will cheer for anything
that lets us own a bit of its victory,
even if it is stricken or so struck
it can't get to the window to wave back
or utter a word to clinch the occasion.

So whether, indeed, his powers of recovery
'confounded his physicians', or with the loss
of finer faculties, as one reported,

he'd 'hardened into dogma', either seemed
to me a daunting prospect: he took on
the character of the headstrong general,
let down, scathing of both sides – but showing
his utmost in the fog and shame of retreat.

And that was when I met him – or, rather,
he allowed me half an hour out of a day.
It was a new thing then, the interview,
brought from America, like women smoking,
but hardly subversive, yet: the courtesies
would still apply, not least in this case.
All morning I'd felt as you do in dreams
when it's time for you to take the penalty,
but the ref has lost the place, the big keeper
keeps stalling, there's a minor crowd invasion,
and even as you begin your run-up a crow
has settled impertinently on the ball;
till at last I was set, after a train down
from Waterloo to Epsom, on the private
crescent of budding limes that led around
to the front of Durdans – his 'out-of-London' house.
It was late April, and a lovely day:
low sun, light wind, daffodils everywhere,
and barely a hint of egg-and-bacon hoops
in the tufts of lambswool cloud that fringed the sky.
Classically fine: but silent, too; as if
the birds had been flushed off the property;
1919, the winter's virus still
camped on the downs, it felt that everything
English was exhausted. Except for this,
which tells you just how far we stood away
from Russia yet: that here, one kind of man

with both his legs, if now lame in the left,
and multiple homes could still expect to bathe
in a freshening pool of national sympathy.
As if we knew, and let it matter, that
he'd been unhappy, in all his place and riches.

Stick to the questions. So I ran them through,
scraping my cane along the sweep of gravel:
*Do you regret your ministry was not*
*a longer one – though so much was achieved?*
*– or, Was it the splits within your own party,*
*or the Irish crisis, more, that brought you down –*
no – *that we should blame the more for your*
*untimely exit?* ('Neither. The truth is,
I had to get out sharp, I was seeing things') –
*And in retirement, what . . .*

                              When in breezed
his amazing daughter. 'How d'ye do!
I'm Peggy Crewe – You must be – Modicum . . .'
– offered her hand, and gave me such a smile
I must have said, indeed I was – I watched
the daisies on her dress – She held her smile;
and as her hand withdrew, I was wondering
at the way this being shone in her station,
whose grace was almost natural, almost
the real thing; and, how I would be the first
to fall in behind her lead or standard –

'But go straight through, he'll be expecting you –
and don't let him start on the spring flowers!'
I barely heard; and then with perfect timing
she'd disappeared. – Yet when I knocked
and entered he was already talking in that
maimed magnificent voice, emphatically, as if

to a nurse or a second invalid concealed
round the dog-leg of the sports or morning room;
to someone who had gone too far
with *primula*, as a name – 'a silly name';
and '*If* I call them primroses, it is
because that is *exactly* what they are.'

# London Scottish

(1914)

April, the last full fixture of the spring:
'Feet, Scottish, feet!' – they rucked the fear of God
Into Blackheath. Their club was everything:
And of the four sides playing that afternoon,
The stars, but also those from the back pitches,
All sixty volunteered for the touring squad,
And swapped their Richmond turf for Belgian ditches.
October: mad for a fight, they broke too soon
On the Ypres Salient, rushing the ridge between
'Witshit' and Messines.      Three-quarters died.

Of that ill-balanced and fatigued fifteen
The ass selectors favoured to survive,
Just one, Brodie the prop, resumed his post.
The others sometimes drank to 'The Forty-Five':
Neither a humorous nor an idle toast.

# Tales of a Grandfather

Like all the braves of Aberdeen, he joined
The 4th Battalion, Gordons.
                                    Whose new gas
Blew back on them at Loos, and got stuck in,
And scorched the whole breathing apparatus.
Speaking by signs and 'faces' after that,
Married, he soldiered on for what was sent –
Four or five operations and a son.
Or that's the story. Maybe it glorifies
What then was a common pulmonary condition.

'He did write once – to the custodians
Of the new memorial, built by subscription,
Up in the castle grounds at Edinburgh,
Which logged the name of every serviceman
Of Scotland killed in the Great War – . . .
He wrote for those who'd lost their former lives
On active duty, but must die civilian.
They answered sympathetically, but stressed
How delicate the task would be to name
Surviving casualties among the dead.'

So says my father – eighty now, who flew
'Ops' in the next – a boy conceived in dread.

## Alex

'Let me guess – light-heavy? The perfect weight,
the Scottish Weight, two hundred pounds,
a hundred in each hand – *bam!* and *bam!*
– a bit of both!'
                            My third night in Alex,
Second at 'Torbit's', the place he ran for men
on a peaceful slip-road just off the waterfront.
Already I am his Scottish Friend, that being
the first thing I would say about myself,
shutting my book . . . . He takes advantage of a lull
to slide his favourite chair up to my table
and starts to kid, that we were what, twin
*pharoes* of granite! in the evening tide
of floaters, that his litter of puppies drew
to take their dinners there; that he had friends,
friends everywhere, in Danzig, Aberdeen,
Smyrna or Mitylene, 'all homes to me',
had made his grid of friends by selling raisins;
that this small trade he did, the meals, would lighten
his retirement, 'make new friends, and help
to make ends meet, oh sure, a bit of that!
But we must let you order . . . *Hakefish?* Could
be good. You might prefer the chops? – Nice choice!
*Hiranthus! Down! Harai!!*
                            What they get now,
Robinson, Patterson . . . – I always say,
boxing was like a school to me, taught me
the ropes, you'd say, the size of the referee.
And best of all was the lesson it meted out
at Hamburg Halle, in nineteen twenty-five.

Just then, I'm making a name, you see, I'm out
from the undercard, the girls are all over me.
Now this old licensee, looked like a reptile,
lived at his desk there, or in a wheelchair,
he made the match for me to fight Iceberg. –
Iceberg. – The guy who'd lost to Johnson – white,
not German – *Bergel*, was it? – in Germany,
but not a German. And he was practically
world champion, just then. Europe at least,
two feet in the House of Fame.
                              Day of the show,
this louse, this lizard guy, he hauls me in,
clips off his big cigar, and says straight out,
Torbit, you won't be going in with the Iceberg –
So I ask, why? – He tells me, the man's dead –
stabbed in the ribs, out in the Spieringstrasse,
heat of an argument – money, a lady –
some yarn. Would you believe it? Never mind,
he says, we've filled his stool for you – sure, a
*third* of the purse. I ask him, what's he like?
He shrugs. Does he care? – Says, he's big, he's thick,
*could be good, could be rubbish*. And that's been
my watchword ever since. This great lump,
I had to hold him up to knock him down,
I never boxed again. You want the lamb?'

## Stuka

While you were down on your hands and knees
Licking my shit off the bowl, Ma,

I made it so we were all sea-falcons
Apart from a few Patagonians, and in the lagoon

Went bobbing for ginger nuts, or scragged
The heads of the flummoxed and flightless scoter.

# Maritime

(1934–67)

*With a few soft words Her Majesty*
Christened the liner built as '504': –
'I name this ship – Myself. God bless . . . .'

The towering masterpiece of the Depression,
She rose from the not-so-bonny Bank of Clyde
(Bombed to a pit for its pains in '41).

Meanwhile, John Masefield wrote a handsome poem
('Shredding a trackway like a mile of snow . . .')
And Harry Lauder roamed the yard with pride.

She ploughed across the Atlantic in four days,
Loud with the 'rich and famous', only the frail
Edwardian Steinways suffering injury

Till Cunard leased her to the cause of war.
We stripped the cabins bare, then stacked them up
With bunks and trunks and barrowloads of boys:

Ten thousand volunteers from New South Wales
And several fifteen-thousands from New York;
Some payload, and she bore it royally.

Winston's flamboyant tribute to 'the Queens'
(She and her sister Elizabeth): 'Their service
Hastened our haul to victory by a year!'

But dear, oh dear, when Cunard got her back,
Her Korkoid floorings marred by a million boots,
It also proved that certain servicemen

Had carved their callow names on the panellings:
'♥ Harvey Woz Ere and hates the lot of you';
'GOD BLESS THIS SHIP AND WALTER DONOGHUE'

⁓

Some queens go on forever: Victoria
And Virgin Bess; others, however buoyant
And bright they seem, succumb before their span.

Queen Mary heard the knell in '49.
Her refit took its bearings from the past,
And while she soldiered on, communal loos

Were deemed 'barbaric' by the new civilian.
The Comet flew; the Ocean turned its back
On an 'ageing Queen' and 'limping Leviathan'.

In '66, the Mary suddenly shook
With strange vibrations; down in the dry dock
They diagnosed a crack in her inner screw –

Inoperable. And the plain verdict came:
'It's Florida or scrap for you, Ma'am . . . .'
They compromised on California.

# Independence

I was about to join you in one of your
suicide forays into the Arab
or Occupied Zone, when I suddenly thought
Why, can't she even blow up on her own?

# Scottish Play

. . . a penny Poet whose first making was the miserable stolne story
of Macdeol, or Macdobeth, or Mac-somewhat, for I am sure a Mac
it was, though I never had the maw to see it . . . .
— WILLIAM KEMP, *Kemp's Nine Days' Wonder*, 1600

Others would rather stammer, and beg your pardon,
Than name that thunderbolt of *opera seria*
Conducted by the 'gentle sorcerer', Gluck,
Which struck the national alto, Kathleen Ferrier,
Although she tweaked the curtain, thrice, for luck
In 1953, at Covent Garden.

A 'wooden actress' – that would be our Kath,
Strumming the plyboard lyre; but when she sang,
So mixed of man and woman, love and death,
Sacred, *heimlich*, and operatic breath,
The house in high forgetfulness forgot
Whom it should mourn or pity, and for what.

And though the wings spared her the customary
Backslap and 'Break a leg!', for her own good,
Her *ca-cancerous* right hip snapped where she stood –
As she recalled in hospital, pillowed and propped
In eiderdown, *I wanted a soft manhole*
*To open up immediately and devour me –*

Still, still, she made them carry her back on stage
To sing his tortured air or aria,
The plum 'Che farò senza Euridice',
Which Gluck implored the original Orfeo,
A bull castrato, to perform 'as if
You're having two-thirds of your leg sawn off'.

[84]

# Domestic

. . . I've been dominated by black aberdeens for some seven years
after nearly 30 dogless ones. Remains now only Malachi (Mike,
Michael, Micky, Don Miguel) – a young 'un with an engaging grin.
   – RUDYARD KIPLING, letter, 1933

It's safe to assume that readers of this book
will know what a Scottish terrier looks like,
the box-faced, low-to-the-ground old dog,
who met with on a shopping expedition
is petted and greeted by every passer-by
as 'Scottie', or 'Jock', or 'Mac'.

Yet the spring of a well-constructed Scot
is still surprising, down on the floor
one minute and up, from a standing start,
on a three-foot-high table the next!
Unresting motion, an eager mien
asking plainly for the word of command;

a muscular form, fit for hard work;
sagacity, nerve, and the wherewithal
to make the most of little: all equip
this breed to be 'Friend of the Family'
or 'Comrade in Arms' more wholly
than any other canine, large or small.

Among his own kind he is peace-loving
and will not pick a quarrel lightly:
but if battle has to be given, he will get hold
and not give in, or let go, for the life of him,
of stick or ball. This huge tenacity
earned him his old title of Diehard.

It is regrettable that no male champion
indicative of Dundee's line has appeared
since Ch. Spofford Dauntless Laddie, born
in 1933. Today there is real doubt
that any dog in direct male descent
from Dundee exists in our country.

I don't know to what breed you refer
   – *Brief Encounter*

## Empty Tumbler

I met in the saloon bar
   A colonel, rheumy-eyed,
Shouting at the batman
   No longer by his side.

Mars without his war-toys
   Was not half so choleric
As that pensioned officer
   Missing his 'Merrick!' –

# Electric Blanket

(1966)

*Oh, that's not in the script!*

It's true, the whole of our street was rooting for Germany –
    West Germany – even my Dad.

After the semi, Sir Alf had said – guarded, as if he were making
    a layman's translation
of soldiering terms, and getting everything wrong but the
    sense – that his novel formation,
this 4-3-3, had 'smothered the Portuguese play at source, like
    an E-lectric blanket' –
which anyone knew, meant Stiles kicking the pants off the
    dark-skinned Eusebio.

But then I had visions of Martin Peters, the one who was
    always 'ahead of his time',
pale as a ghost at night, going through the doors and private
    rooms of an old people's home
and striking softly, before their fingers could close on the
    'help' bulb or the bedside light;

or, I might wake in the wet at the thought of the Glasgow
    polis entering mine, a couple
of Roger Hunts in pursuit of a misprint – the boy in this very
    bed who was heard to be
*warming his lions* – as if he had three of them cubs stitched
    to the plaque of his Y-Fronts.

# Overprotected

Yes, but when Uncle Frank,
an outlaw by our standards,
confided in me once
about *the kind of boy*
*whose main concern's to cover*
*his own* A, R, S, E
– he spelt it, so my parents
wouldn't be able to hear it,
and I was thrilled to bits.

In *Model Soldier Monthly*
we tugged the rug from under
Revel's 'Roman *Testudo*':
'The model is basically solid,
a block of resin with shields
carved over five sides;
the gamer is thus unable
to enact the unit's collapse, or
by extension a Roman defeat.

'*Testudo* is moving forward,
so the men's feet are visible,
as are the tops of their helmets.
In addition, one man is peering
out through the roof of shields:
he may be the "eyes" of the unit,
but looks far too tall, or
as if he's recently opened
the hatch on some antique tank.

'*Testudo* might be exposed
by modern weapons, a hazard
explored in a future issue.
Meanwhile, this schoolboy howler.
As well as shields on top,
to front and sides, this lot
have shields to the rear – redundantly
aimed at their own (unless
they knew something we don't!).

'But seriously, this structure
would not have worked in the field,
as four new men would be needed
to carry the rear guard, stretching
the "flesh" of the so-called tortoise
beyond the rim of the shell.
Besides, how would they look,
these "tail-end Charlies", in skirts
and open sandals, straining

to shift ahead, while their arms
were bent to clamp the protection
on their buttocks and bare calves? . . .
*Conclusion*: our copy
had numerous ugly clots
of resin that called for trimming.
The rear shields (see above)
should not be there. Otherwise
a useful piece. Three stars.'

# Starter's Orders

(*Ale. In this land*
*No man has hired us.*
*Our life is unwelcome, our death*
*Unmentioned in* The Times.)

These warless days
Men without women
Thirst for a way
To waste themselves;

It's in the blood.
Their fathers worked
And Grandad breasted
A barbed tape;

But now where the girls
Are sick of courage
Men without hope
Of a job or a bayonet

Muster like champions
Under a canopy,
Over a barrel,
Primed for the slaughter,

Fit to pursue
Illness, dishonour,
And sponsored to boot.
Gentlemen, swallow!

## The Bright Side

Ach, don't keep on
At the seaside Scot
For his daytime drinking;
Better than not.

Look on the bright side.
Think of the future;
Picture a ghost
With a hand like paper

Pegging you back with
'Hi, I'm Mac –
A reformed alcoholic!'
(Ghastly, earnest) –

Picture his eyes
(Pin-clear, pleading),
Think of a night
Like a Bible Reading –

And view the unseasonal
Clown on the pier
('I only get drunk, ooh,
Twice in the year –

Hic! – Tober to May,
And May to October!')
In kindlier light
(At least he's not sober).

# Drink v. Drugs

I was worked up about some other matter
when I saw that phone box off the Talbot Road
being smashed outwards by someone inside it,
after closing on Sunday (Sunday's the day
they all go mad on crack); which is why
I didn't as usual walk by on the other side
but advanced with a purpose, and as he swivelled
nonchalant out of the frost, grabbed his lapels,
and setting him roughly against the railings,
'What is it with you,' I asked him, 'drugs?' –

which I knew very well from his vacant expression;
and after he'd cautioned me weakly
against tearing his coat, the stoned boy
answered, matter-of-factly, 'Yes' –
and told me which ones, in a Liverpool accent.
It was here I think I said something stupid
about rugby v. football, which he ignored,
rallying rather to call me a prick
and a Good Citizen, and I thought, never mind,
I'm still going to call the police.

But that would have meant myself going into
the vandalised box, and releasing my hold,
which maybe he saw, with his pert 'Go on then';
then, something better came into his head,
that *he* would phone, since he hadn't done nothing;
and moments later he was giving the station
the lowdown on the guy in a light blue shirt
and black jeans who'd assaulted him, seeming
the worse for drink, and accused me of smashing
the phone box from which he was calling now.

[93]

When in fact I'd begun to warm to the lad –
who'd flattered my stab at authority, kept
a lid on the thing; also I couldn't be sure,
could I, that he hadn't been simply clearing away
glass that was broken already, with strong
but not violent blows of the phone.
In any case, when he started to amble off,
I did nothing to stop him; and when the blue
light came quietly round the corner I was standing
alone with nothing to say for myself but my name.

# Past Caring

As a ship
Sees only the tip
Of the ice's pyramid
That has already scraped her bows,
We'd glimpsed that drink was something you overdid;
Now after the wreck I sift the damage you'd stowed in the house.

Eyes glazed
I fumble, amazed,
Through mounds of knickers and slips,
Extracting the bottles you'd buried there; these
I hump in their binbags, clashing against my knees
To the 'bottle bank', by the public baths; it takes four trips.

The gin!
No wonder you're thin;
Hundreds of bottles of gin;
And feeding them singly into the ring
My arm grows weary from shifting the bottles of gin;
A numbing collection of lots of exactly the same thing.

You were vain
As you went down the drain;
Why else would you lay up this hoard
If it wasn't one day to take stock as I'm doing
Of what an almighty amount you had taken on board?
And here am I turning your trophies to scrap at an illicit viewing!

A smear
Of lipstick, here –
Like the kiss on a valentine;
And sniffing the neck I feel suddenly near to you,
For what it gives off is your smell, if we kissed any time,
And it wasn't a cheap perfume – but the only thing properly dear
    to you.

Next week
If you're not past caring
They may let you out for an airing,
To slump in your armchair, too burgled to speak,
The fish out of water that stubbornly stays all the more fish:
Then how shall we drag the treasure you were back to the surface

# Stephen Boyd

(1957–99)

*And on thai went, talkand of play and sport . . .*
    – HENRYSON, *Orpheus and Eurydice*

I can't drive, and I dreamt that I was driving
Unstoppably through a succession of red lights
Till I hit that slow moving Transit amidships –
A crash that must elsewhere have killed somebody.
So I was doubly relieved, when the smoke cleared,
To see it was you who climbed unhurt from the van,
Fuming: you, who I knew to be dead already;
For though the SALTIRE overlaid your face,
The funeral mask of Scotland's Everyman,
Those specs and spry moustache gave you away –
Those, and the warmth in your abuse of me –
And it seemed from how your empty trousers scissored
And slipped through the ground, the dream after all
Was benign; they'd made you a sort of wizard.

I first ran into you in '82,
In Oxford, when you came over the road
From a rival college, to do graduate work
In Magdalen MCR: four pints a night,
Electric-thin, brimful of mimicry,
With a laugh that stopped unnervingly – .
We might have kept suspiciously apart:
You a Glaswegian from the Irish side;
Me, from the softer suburbs of the Kirk,
Who hadn't knowingly met a Catholic boy
Till I was sent to have my tonsils out
In the Ear, Nose and Throat on the Paisley Road

Aged seven, where the alien ward was full
Of green favours, Celtic scarfs and scruffs;
And years of a Southern education since
Had trimmed my Scottishness to a tartan phrase
Brought out on match days and Remembrance Days.

So football, I'd assumed, would be your game –
Not the perversion I was public-schooled in;
Until, one evening's ending at the bar,
Jocking it up, I 'prophesied' aloud
The 'greatness' of some teenage Border prospect,
Saviour of Scottish rugby and so on –
And you stepped out of the wan group you'd adopted,
With that particular look you had, half doubt,
Half reckless allegiance; the look, in fact,
Of the early Christian in the film *The Robe*,
Patrolling Nero's streets, when his ear catches
In a slave's whistle from the sewer beneath
A Hebrew melody gone underground:
The trace-note of some fellow in the faith.

Those days, the Scots lost more games than they won,
But the playing parts were mightier than the sum:
The last sparks of the cherub Andy Irvine,
My mother's favourite, 'out of Heriot's';
The hooker, Deans, pent-up, belligerent;
The steep kicks of our fly-half, Rutherford
('That one's come down with snow on it, I'll tell you');
Paxton the number eight, who on the box
Was always 'thumping on' or 'smashing on';
And Leslie, the deadly flanker from Dundee.
You also liked that Catholic lump from Hawick,
Shonnie McGaughey, who in the national side
Revelled in having bridged the great divide.

This is a long poem for a friendship based
On little more than aping Bill McLaren,
And spelling out again that sport matters
Because it doesn't matter; by such a ruse,
If not for long, worse things could be postponed. –
Meanwhile, two prigs, we liked to disapprove
Of those who showed their fears or bared their heart;
As when, in one of your fancier flights,
You said of the social posture of a scholar
Whose girlfriend had gone off with someone other,
That he 'expects the whole community
To circulate his sorrow, open-mouthed,
Like the wee Marys in Giotto's *Crucifixion*!'

The problem was, that day in late November,
When flu had scrubbed out half of Magdalen's strength,
To get fifteen of any ability out
To take on Balliol; when you piped up
Unhelpfully, 'I'll play' – yet there was no one else.
So we put you at full-back, farthest away
From the kick-off, at least; you had arrived
In a pair of khaki shorts (we played in black),
Which in a private reference to the kilt
You wore with nothing underneath, and kept
Your heavy-duty glasses on as well;
I'm sorry, but you looked ridiculous.
Ten minutes in, nil-nil, my hamstring went,
And we were down to fourteen – or, thirteen
Plus you. And yet, although you couldn't 'catch
To save your life', today you rescued Magdalen.
You pouched their box-kick with a booming 'Mark!',
Tackled and got to your feet and tackled again,
Swearing in Scots, and in attack made one

Comedian's charge through their amazed three-quarters.
I thought you'd crack in the second half; you didn't;
Not when a bonfire spread the field with smoke,
Or the light faded, towards the final whistle.
Six-three to us: a try by David Gearing.
Now I pull muscles sprinting in my sleep
And you make probing runs from the deeper deep.

Two white diagonals on a field of blue:
The Saltire, or the *crux decussata*,
Banner of *Braveheart* and the Glasgow Kiss,
Is said to represent the wooden X
To which, one morning by the harbourfront
At Patras, they attached our patron saint,
The first disciple, Andrew of Galilee,
Fisher of Men, called 'Manly' in the Greek:
Then seventy, a good age for a martyr.
We see it in the struts of a hurdle gate;
We saw it in the angles on the blackboard
Of the attacking full-back and his wing
When scissoring or dummy-scissoring.

A warm deceptive spring followed the March
Of David Sole's Grand Slam in 1990;
I flew up to St Andrews, where you'd won
A fellowship in English, and got married
To Sue the musician; since somehow you'd fixed it
For the powers-that-be up there to pay me
To do a poetry reading with Kathleen Jamie.
Our lives had changed, or yours had changed especially,
But still we had our taste for the old routine;
In the Indian afterwards, you leant forward
To murmur, like an arch-conspirator,
'I predict greatness for Damian Cronin' –

A good hard lock, though frequently overweight,
In and out of the side till his knee gave way
In '98 – and never quite as good as great.

Of all your flawed predictions, this was the last,
That I remember. Soon we'd got the bus
Back to the pretty house you'd bought in Crail,
A fishing village with a postcard harbour,
And hit the whisky, you harmlessly hammered
In front of your wife; till the turning point
The pleasure ended, or pretending did.
You'd put a record on, of Monteverdi,
Or something even earlier, singing yourself
In a passionate, reedy voice – and weeping, lots,
Then weeping more; and Sue had arms around you,
Stroking and shooshing, but without surprise –
So this was not the first time, nor the last.
She made you steady, and I went to bed,
And slept; but it resumed—whispers, breaking –
You exclaiming – she hushing you down –
And when she brought my morning tea, you'd gone.

I heard you had two boys ('just thirteen more . . .'),
But didn't write; and then your colleague phoned
To say he understood that we'd been close
(I heard you bristle back, 'We were *not close*'),
And that he was afraid you'd 'Taken Your Life' –
Preferring not to say in which specific
Knock-kneed, hurtful, individual style.
*It doesn't matter*. And I wouldn't force the door
For one cartoon, Body with rocks, bottles,
Or railway track, to blot out what you were;
But while we're at it, I'd be pleased to know
Your standpoint on the new Cronin, Scott Murray,

Whose jumping in the line-out begs comparison
With the Spey salmon; and to square with you
The lessons I was meant to take away
From our phantom collision: not to let die
The memory of your glorious afternoon
V. Balliol; and not to dwell on loss
If your sons' path and mine should ever cross.

# Gordon Brown

(Rugby player – 'The Ayrshire Bull' – d. 2001)

Their gratitude for your career was such
That when some District prop in his narrow pride
Stamped on your head, and legged it into touch,
The Board banned *you* (that's rugby suicide):
Who blew through London Scottish on the breeze,
When I'd been training with the fourths or thirds
And dreamt you said *I'd like to meet him, please!*,
Till someone drew me in, and we had words.

You knew two bits of Burns. Still you pretended
Poems would outlast what the British Lions did,
You, who had beaten Springbok and All Black;
And when you put your spare hand on my back
I felt at first a woman, then a kid,
And then a man, the thing you had intended.

*Citizens of Sparta who remained unmarried after a certain age suffered various penalties. They were not allowed to witness the gymnastic exercises of the maidens; and during winter they were compelled to march naked round the market-place, singing a song composed against themselves and expressing the justice of their punishment.*

## Dad's Army

When the doctor issues the all-clear,
that hurts you, too – winched of a sudden
from setting your mine under the march

of union, and told with a grin, *for you,*
*the war is over; besides, it was never,*
*you're going to discover, a war at all*;

i. e., there isn't a role for you, mate,
but to play the shamed veteran,
the dazed repugnant Lazarene,

to go back as one in the Doric,
literally *raised from his bed*,
to the nothing you've made of it . . .

So you lug your pack through beanfields
on either side, through one encounter
with a family scout, the kid on recce

who hails you, *hey!*, with a mirthless play
on your Spartan name, combining
the words for wild boar and backrub,

till there, on a facing slope, is your old
grey house, the same – but different; white;
someone has been painting it.

~

The crossroads, and a posse of village
women is out – acting as if they've put
their heads together over a cooking-pot

and ventured to shake some sense in now
along with their revelation; she, more lenient
or closely related than some of her neighbours,

saying, 'I wouldn't go up directly – it's just
that while you were off on your wargames –'
(someone behind her, *the fool, he ought*

*to look after his own*) ' – a German has stolen
under your lintel, and knocked you up
some eggs and a pair of *flachsenkinder.*'

# Maren

You saw so much romance in competition,
like Atalanta before you – daughter
of thick-witted Schoeness, a Boeotian –
they said you'd marry anyone who beat you
in a footrace. Hence our peculiar courtship:

you, crowned once the fastest girl over
three thousand metres in Lower Franconia,
myself the great Caledonian bore,
we took to jogging round the astroturf
of Wapping's amenable sports arena.

Plainly, you could have romped ahead
at any point; instead, you made me lead,
woman after my own heart! – dropping
your courteous metres back, as if
feeling the pace, an arrangement

you gilded with 'I can't keep up
when you accelerate!' So we complete
our sixth or seventh lap of the course;
and only when I flag, an end in view,
near to the bags and coats, do you appear

flush at my ear, demanding 'more!'
Together, then, after our fashion:
exchanging oaths like old antagonists,
your Focke-Wulf tailing my Spit
into fresh air and another orbit.

# Iona

*Where are you taking us, sir?*
the crew needed to know;
but since by the final day
    my guiding star,
instinct and purpose both, had strayed so far
off the monitor – I found I couldn't stay
    for fear of the answer.

    To tell the truth
I had given up on youth; would only stew
in the chemical toilet, the door half-
open, a 'cry for help', till out of the blue
    a nurse ducked
from the cockpit holding you, and I
was face to face with my pilot!

      ~

In the weeks before you were born
    the head did warn
me not to give over the stage at once
to baby talk: and so we stood our ground
when from among your breathings-out were told
    two voluntary sounds,
a rudimentary yes and no.

But now, when all the words
we care about are yours, I have to tender
    our deep surrender;
as in a suit of dungarees you go
    groping your way to sense
like Milton, blind before he felt
    the wall's resistance.

Already you discern what the artist meant
in an old poster of mine, the 'Mars'
of Velazquez: the war god in his afterprime
    released too soon
from that perpetual service; sat
in his demob nakedness and gloom,
only his helmet on, almost
a souvenir, muscles smoking away,
    until you up and say
– *Poor tin soldier man!*
*He's thinking about things*!

~

My right hand is Nessie's head,
her neck my dripping arm. *How old*
*is the dinosaur?* Forty
    or fifty million years.
*Can the dinosaur sing?* No,
too old; but likes to be soothed
    by others singing.

I open her thumb-
    and-finger beak
at least to let her speak
in her quavery Triassic,
'Take me to your leader!'
– to which you instantly,
    *I haven't got any leader.*

~

What, meanwhile, are my own terms?
Darling – 'little' – *Mädchen* – the same
Suspicious argot I used to spy on.

∾

Strange, that we dwell so much
sometimes, on self and such,
that we can spend an age without
    a clear view out:
when, if I asked the mirror once
in the way of an old queen,
to frame how things might look
twenty or thirty visits thence,
all it reflected back was white
and unrefracted light, the mean
prophetics of a closed book.

Of course, it was not allowed to show
    or we to know
that you were coming all the time,
    my perfect rhyme;
how you would seize the reins, Iona,
riding my shoulders over the hill
    or rarely sitting still,
your hands spread on my knees, my jeans
    the sidelines of your throne.
Succession is easy: first it was them,
then me for a bit; and now it's you.

∾

Granted your repertoire
    has lumps in it,
of Shrek and Cinderella;
but there's prodigious poetry too,
    a magic spring
in the sweet Cordelia thing
you once undid me with –

*Let's laugh through all the days, till the water*
    *comes over our eyes . . .*
or, which is more my line – not
mawkish, I think, or maudlin:
*In Oxford Church, there are two Marys;*
    *one of them has got a baby*
*and one of them hasn't got a baby.*

1  In Memoriam Alfred Lord Tennyson

(d. 6 October 1892)

> I remember once in London the realization coming over me, of the
> whole of its inhabitants lying horizontal a hundred years hence.
>     – TENNYSON, quoted in Audrey Tennyson's notebook

No one remembers you at all.
    Even that shower of Cockney shrimps
    Whose fathers hoisted them to glimpse
Your corpse's progress down Whitehall

Have soiled the till and lain beneath
    While the last maid you kissed with feeling
    Is staring at the eternal ceiling
And has no tongue between her teeth.

Now sanctified are your remains:
    The poems; Hallam's obedient book;
    The photographs your neighbour took
Of an old Jesus with food stains;

The rest is dressed up decently
    And drowned, as surely as your son's
    Untimely coffin, that flashed once
And slipped into the Indian Sea.

You are not here; you cannot fall.
    So let the mighty organ blare!
    While we, who plainly were not there
Construct this fake memorial.

In the hope of finding something that might flesh out my phantom Tennyson Centenary project, my girlfriend drove me one evening down to Aldworth in Sussex, the poet's second home and the closest of his haunts to London. We had read of the new owner's excessive hostility to visitors, but she wasn't deterred, on my behalf, by the height of the gate or by the notice of watchdogs. So I followed her suggestion to break into the garden, and carried the torch down a path which gave me a dim view of the front of the house, from about fifty metres, across a minefield of lilies and a steaming pond, and absorbed this for a minute before heading back to join her on the drive. But even as my feet landed again on common gravel, she screamed – not at the flash of what seemed like theatrical lightning but at something on my blind side it must have lit up. So I turned to confront what I guessed in that instant was either our man with a shotgun or an earlier intruder strung up by his heels.

≈

Cannot you, as a friend of Mr Tennyson, prevent his making such a hideous exhibition of himself as he has been doing for the last three months? . . . I thought there was a law against indecent exposure.
   – SWINBURNE to Lord Houghton

When fifteen men were charged at Bow Street Court on Monday after a disturbance around Eros, in Piccadilly Circus, it was mentioned in court that one of them claimed to be Lord Tennyson. Lord Tennyson wishes to state that the man was not in fact Lord Tennyson, and has no connections with him, and that he does not know him.
   – The Times, 1 January 1948

≈

I knew him at once – for a student, or out-of-work actor, or
    worse,
With Tennyson's frock and fedora, and a volume of Tennyson's
    verse,
But even the mouldiest music-hall turn would be sunk from the
    start
By a stature at least seven inches too short for the laureate's part.
This was a bloke whose Kraken had woken for years twice a
    night
In some shallow provincial canal; and when he began to recite,
The personal touch of the door-to-door salesman could never
    obscure
That this was the fiftieth one-to-one Tennyson show of the tour.
'Mr Imlah! The warmest of greetings, good sir, from myself and
    the Queen!
I'm Alfred, Lord Tennyson – dare I suggest that you know who
    I mean?
So relax – and unlock the front gates of your mind – for tonight
    I arrive
To proclaim as I did once before – The Dead Are Not Dead But
    Alive!'

∼

. . . the full, the monstrous demonstration that Tennyson was not
Tennysonian
        – HENRY JAMES, *The Middle Years*

(Oscar Browning introduces himself):
O. BROWNING: I am Browning.
TENNYSON: No you're not.
        – E. F. BENSON, *As We Were*

This is the most extraordinary drawing. It is exactly like myself.
        – TENNYSON on a portrait of the dead Dickens

∼

'The trick of the afterlife is – that what you sign up for, you get,
Which as in the case of Tithonus, we have leisure enough to
    regret.
Ours is a sepia parlour, a club without pipes or the port,
Half full of identical males, where Her Majesty still holds court.
As we strut in our standardised jacket, beards on our
    standardised face,
Dickens and Grace and myself are dubbed the Three Graces –
    by Grace.
There isn't a future in Heaven; no nightclub, or pool with
    jacuzzi –
You walk in the garden with Gladstone, or stand at the piano
    with Pusey.
And yet, while we keep the old pastimes, we keep the old
    dread:
And that, for our sins, is an absolute terror of being dead.
These days we can hardly get four for bridge; I've seen the
    departure
Of Lytton – accepted – but *Manning*, by God, and Macaulay,
    and *Archer!*
They're all cast over the margin and into the beggarly throng
Who bray for biography, down in the darkness, all the night
    long.
My Arthur – poor angel, I did what I could – I see in fits:
His wings gone limp with disuse, and the plumage in ribbons
    where bits
Of his carcass stick out like spokes of a battered and bandaged
    umbrella.
His features appear where he gnaws at the grille of his terrible
    cellar,
Fading and growing and fading again with never a sound,
And but for my friendship his luminous half-life would choke
    underground.

'Tonight there was dancing in heaven – jigs with Elizabeth
    Siddall.
But after an hour on the fringe of events, and her in the middle,
I suddenly hated the uniform steps and the scrape of the fiddle,
And staggered out dizzily into the thick of the alien stars,
Shouting my name, till Hesperus fetched me in one of her cars
And dropped me on Earth for the evening. I'm saved. And to
    hell with the distance –
There's times when you've got to get out amongst folk to
    promote your existence.'

And now from the folds of his frock coat he conjured the
    book, and affected
A cartoon myopia, cribbed from its cover (the Penguin
    *Selected*),
'And so to that end it's my pleasure to read to you – starting
    with: *Maud*.
I hate –' But I couldn't take more of this – be it dementia, or
    fraud,
So I hushed him abruptly and fished out a quid for the
    in-patients' kitty
And gathered my girlfriend to make our way back to her car
    and the city,
Casting a jibe at him over my shoulder – 'You're not Lord
    Tennyson!' –
Catching the small, disembodied retort, 'Well, neither's Lord
    Tennyson.'

~

Tennyson at a seance –
A great poet, lest we forget,
And certainly one of the most haunted –
Before all the others had settled,
Cried out in a cracked voice,
'Are you my boy Lionel?'
And got
Not
The reply that he wanted.

## II 'B.V.'

If circumstances had been smoother and brighter about him . . . he
would have had what was much needed in his case, a more spacious
home.
          – GEORGE MEREDITH, letter to Henry Salt, 1 September 1888

## The Walker

Had I but means and a free mind
    You'd never tie me to one bed
For I should wander unconfined
    And virgin paths should feel my tread
        – JAMES THOMSON, unpublished fragment, Dobell MS


Things being worse, while I must creep
    Each evening back to Pimlico
Still I can leap before I sleep
    Through Hampstead Heath, or Barnes, or Bow,

Unless THE CLOUD resume its place
    And the rains rain gutterly;
For then I pace my given space –
    Three by four, four by three –

And feel akin to the caged creatures
    In Regent's Park: to the roofed-in
Eagle with the impacted features,
    Or the brown bear in his bear-bin

Who rocks upon a yard of slate
    With room for three of his four paws,
Shifting his weight to simulate
    The bearing of the thing he was.

## An Invitation

Kirby Muxloe, Leics.

Friend, come and stay awhile; Miss Barrs and I
    Crave the refreshment of your company;
And if, of late, your old unhappiness
    Has made you sick, better to convalesce
Where we can nourish you with country things,
    Like Leicester beans and bacon – 'food of kings',
And the best smell the subject ever smelt;
    Pork pies from Melton Mowbray, pies that melt,
Crust, meat, and jelly, in the crowded mouth;
    Pickles from Branston Valley to the south;
Stilton, or *Quenby*, judged 'the greatest cheese
    In all the world' by local authorities;
And the fat capon from the farmyard, done
    In wine and lemon – or lemon and tarragon.
Thence to the [non-!] smoking room, where we may pass
    Hours with the couplet rather than the glass,
And put old Horace right ('No poem lasts long
    That hath been writ on *aqua*' – doubly wrong,
Steeped as he was in the Pierian Spring);
    And last, with nightcaps on our heads, we'll sing
Accompanied purely by my father's daughter,
    To prove the lyric qualities of water.

Homely amusements! – and they may read mild
    To one whose nature has run wholly wild;
But look: we have a thousand acres here
    Of fern and gorse, and ancient oak, and deer,
To ramble where you will; and in such grounds
    Your spirit may shake off the ghostly hounds

That haunt you into illness. Come, be calm;
    Do odd jobs, if you like, around the farm,
Feeding the chickens, or collecting wood;
    And if your pledge of abstinence holds good,
The Fates may yet extend their benisons
    And *Thomson*'s star be twinned with *Tennyson*'s
A hundred years from now. So come, my friend,
    As soon as possible; come next weekend,
When Harry's children will be up with him –
    Who love you, James, as much as you love them.

     – J. W. BARRS to James Thomson, 28 March 1882

      ~

Sir,
    You will appreciate that your presence is no longer to be tolerated in this house. Since your own apparatus will doubtless be unable to reconstruct the events of the early hours of this morning, I should record: i) that earlier in your stay Miss Barrs had discovered flasks of what we take to be brandy concealed in the outbuildings – ii) that you went out with your pipe after supper and – despite our search and shouted entreaties – did not return at least until after we retired which was as late as midnight – and iii) your worse than nauseous condition – *before the children* – when you at last unlocked your door this morning – which, taken together, prove your vow broken and our trust betrayed, – with what dreadful consequences.
    As you pertly said before you disappeared, you cannot, with your means, hope to make recompense for the loss of 200 fowl, or for the damage the fire has done to the brooder house. Neither is it meaningful to 'thank' us for past kindnesses, as if these should be endlessly repeated. I cannot wish you ill, only that you were better. But I despair of you.

     – J. W. BARRS, draft of letter, spring 1882; not sent

~

Nowhere is the verse feeble . . . the majesty of the line always has its full colouring, and marches under a banner. And you accomplish this effect with the utmost sobriety, with absolute self-mastery.

    – GEORGE MEREDITH, letter to James Thomson, 27 April 1880

No news—except that he is still on the warpath and in very full paint.

    – H. HOOD BARRS, Letter to J. W. Barrs, 17 April 1882

~

Dear Mr Barrs,
                Alas! – I'm afraid I was squiffy myself,
When I offered to ride to his rescue. – Still, I was hot on the scent;
For I followed that dog-eared stub of address to a Pimlico
    roomhouse,
In the shade of railbridge spattered by pigeons, and rapped at
    the door
At nine in the morning on Monday – the likeliest hour of the
    week.

The landlord is GIBSON, an irascible type with an air of long
    suffering,
Who as I pronounced the offending initials stepped back with
    a snort –
And then, with sarcastic good manners, conducted me through
    to the scullery,
Where *guess what* had happened – the walls scorched, the floor
    awash
With charred rags, and chairlegs, and offal and cabbage, all
    sodden and sooty.

It appears that at five this Gibson had woken with smoke in his
    nostrils
And stumbled downstairs, grabbing at buckets of slop as he went,
To discover a fairsized bonfire ablaze in the heart of his kitchen,

And our hero, impassively viewing the scene from the warmth
    of an armchair,
Offering never a word of excuse – only after a while,

And then, very often, shouting out 'Heebson! *Olé! Olé!*
*Señor Heebson! Olé!* – alluding, I learned, to a wild
But unshakeable fancy of his that the landlord was secretly
    *Spanish*.
(*For reference* – it seems the said Spaniard had dared in the
    earlier evening
Engage with his crapulous lodger on matters of *rent* – hence this.)

So Gibson had chucked him out 'sharp', and was voluble now
    in relief,
Being rid of that 'stink', as he put it, for good – crowing,
    indeed,
That if ever that 'B—' should darken his doorstep again, by
    G—d,
He could count on a merry reception, etc. I bid him good day
And was happy for that to remain the extent of our novel
    acquaintance . . .

But I hadn't been home for an hour, when Gibson came
    knocking at *mine* –
For listen – the whole of the time he'd been cursing the fellow
    to hell
B.V. had been upstairs asleep, in one of the unlet rooms!
Since G. in the heat of his temper had failed to recover *the key* –
Our Homer had simply slipped in while he fumed at his coffee
    and kippers!

This time, he went meekly, it seems – though leaving his mark
    on the bed –
Remembering, he claimed, that he'd business to see to, with
    'friends in the park'

Which G. took to mean with 'his brethren, them beasts what
   they keep behind bars'.
Since then, I report, no one's seen hide nor hair of him –
   living or dead –
Including
            Yours Truly
                     I wish I was sorry to say.

   – PERCY HOLYOAKE to J. W. Barrs, 17 April 1882

   ∾

'He's been taken very ill,' I urged. 'He can do no harm now. Won't
you take him in if we bring him?' The man emphasized his refusal
with an oath, and slammed the door.
   – T. E. CLARKE, account of events of 1 June 1882

With money, I believe I should never have a home, but be always
going to and fro the earth, and walking up and down in it.
   – JAMES THOMSON in conversation

   ∾

## The Library

GENTLEMEN ARE REMINDED
THE READING ROOM IS NOT A HOSTEL
on barred doors, at midnight;
beside it, LIVE THIS EVENING:
THE AUTHOR OF 'INSOMNIA',
'THE WALKER', 'IN MY ROOM', ETC. –

the very man who now hogged the portal, –
head first, as if to butt in five hours late
on his own abandoned reading,
but not so much as breathing
through the mask of custard, brandy, blood
his spatchcock nose had blurted.

Yet stooping as I did
to find what work-in-progress
had stopped in those pockets,
the eyes in the back of my head
detected a thing less dead, –
a statue, hard by –

a stray from the museum:
but on its brow, there blew a live
crown of leaves; and the wind's pulse
rippled its grooves of gown;
and when its finger moved to fix
the wet clay I straightened from,

a stone voice ground out at me
(in English, with a marble accent),
'Relieve yourself, now, on this head's flesh,
The quicker to melt it into mulch and aether –'
(so anxious to obey, I looked to see
I was already doing as he instructed)

'– For a reputation spoils in the stacks
With fox marks on the pages, and this
Oaf's glandular grin for a frontispiece:
This northern appetite – this *bon viveur* –
This bear-faced bevvying barnacle –
"B.V.", as he would have me style my poems.

'An umpteenth birthday passed in a cage of rain;
My small perennial hopes – a collie, and heather,
And Harriet Barrs – were ash in the grate again;
So when he knocked and wheedled and begged and beavered
And roared to have our head, my self was spent,
And he dissolved us in his element.

'But leave that – since the terms of my new estate
Are to walk as I have never walked before!'
So we did walk: he streets ahead, composing
a queer Senecan hopscotch, or drifting
beside me in companionable silence;
until the dark began to fade.

Then he pulled up, as if short of breath,
and seemed to be sweating, and needed a shave,
and offered his empty hand in a hurry,
'I leave the card of *The Rambler* magazine,
as I cannot be sure of my present address
for some time to come,' and was nothing.

NOTE: *The story of the poet James Thomson (1834–82), author of* The City of Dreadful Night, *is told in Tom Leonard's book* Places of the Mind. *Thomson was born in Port Glasgow but removed aged six to London, where he was educated in an institution for Scottish orphans. An alcoholic, he was 'discharged with disgrace' from his first post as an army schoolmaster, and thereafter lived as a lodger in a succession of single rooms in Pimlico, scraping an irregular income from contributions to journals like* Cope's Tobacco Plant. *He never published under his own name, preferring the pseudonym 'B.V.' and in one fit of self-disgust burned all his personal papers as he approached what he wrongly thought was the midpoint of his life, his thirty-fifth birthday. Twelve years on, offered a belated chance by friends, the Barrs (two brothers and a sister) to recover himself in the Leicestershire countryside, he relapsed instead into one last 'dreadful night' in the city, and died of a broken blood vessel in his bowel a few weeks later. He was an uncompromising free-thinker, and a constant theme of his serious verse is the impossibility of an afterlife.*

## III

> ...which have no memorial, who are perished as though they had never bene
>> – Ecclesiasticus

> Tonight I saw, concerning the Milky Way – a phenomenon we have understood as a form of a vapour, raised to reflect the glow of the stars in their houses – this contrary characteristic: it is crowded, and each part crowded again, with its own infinitely progenitous rabble of living stars. Neither – unless it were calculated elsewhere that we should devise such a chamber of lenses as is our instrument today, by the seemingly random  development of optical science in Antwerp – is this rude theatre set up for the instruction or amusement of mankind. For my observation suggests what may be impossible to conceive except by figure or metaphor: that our Zodiac is like a false vault in the cellar of Babel: whose brightest lights, in the vast upstairs, would disappear.
>> – GALILEO, Notebooks, 12 June 1611

It's a free-for-all. Vandals have shattered the Sistine ceiling
and pitched the creator down on the midden with Castor and
    Pollux;
and the notes of the scale are heard no more, nor lanterns
    seen
than the holes between; or the wide estates between holes,
where heaven's unlikely guest revolves at his massive leisure
or bores his way through sleeps of aether; where the worst,
    fractious
asteroid beams in her thousand miles of cold dominion.

And fair play to rejects – to busts with broken noses –
whose last great work was finding a shed or a stable to die in,
if they dream away their loss of face in a sky like that;
if there, though day's glare or the northern night obscure
    them,

though nature has done with them, still through the void they
   hurtle their wattage,
powered with the purpose of having been – being, after all,
   stars,
whose measure we may not take, nor know the wealth of
   their rays.